Trending Toward Cultural Captivity

Learning to Survive the Inevitable

James Perry

Trending Toward Cultural Captivity

Copyright © 2014 by James Perry

Published by: Theocentric Publishing Group
1069A Main Street
Chipley, Florida 32428

http://www.theocentricpublishing.com

All rights reserved. No part of this book may be reproduced or transmitted in any form or by any means without written permission of the author

Library of Congress Control Number: 2014948473

ISBN 9780991481149

Scriptural Citations

Unless otherwise noted, the Scriptural Quotations are taken from the American Standard Version (1901). This Bible is in the public domain in the United States.

Other Versions Used

The New King James Version (NKJV), © 1982 by Thomas Nelson, Inc. All rights reserved. Used within Guideline Permission.

The Holy Bible, English Standard Version® (ESV®) Copyright © 2001 by Crossway. Used within Guideline Permission.

New International Version, THE HOLY BIBLE, NEW INTERNATIONAL VERSION®, NIV® Copyright © 1973, 1978, 1984, 2011 by Biblica, Inc.™ All rights reserved worldwide. Used within Guideline Permission.

New Living Translation (NLT), Scripture quotations are taken from the *Holy Bible*, New Living Translation, copyright ©1996, 2004, 2007, 2013 by Tyndale House Foundation. Used within Guideline Permission of Tyndale House Publishers, Inc., Carol Stream, Illinois 60188.

The Message (MSG), *The Message*. Copyright © 1993, 1994, 1995, 1996, 2000, 2001, 2002. Used within Guideline Permission of NavPress Publishing Group.

Other scant references are taken from Williams Translation of the New Testament; J. B. Philipps Translation of the New Testament; and The Amplified Bible. Used within Guideline Permission.

Acknowledgements and Dedications

Paul stated in I Corinthians 15:10 (NLT): "But whatever I am now, it is all because God poured out his special favor on me--and not without results. For I have worked harder than any of the other apostles; yet it was not I but God who was working through me by his grace."

Particular experiences, people and places influence and contribute to who a person is and what he becomes. As a boy and young man, a small group called the Gospel Meeting House gave me the opportunity to participate in ministry. They had a church band and not only did they teach us how to learn an instrument, but they let us play it in the church meeting. Even though a mistake may have been made in what was done, another opportunity would be given to try once again.

Through the Lakeside Bible Conference Summer ministry, I was given opportunities to learn and do things in different areas. The Director of the Camp Program was a godly man who saw the potential in those who were just aimlessly wandering through life. At that Camp, I met people who were a positive influence. It was because of a summer experience that I would be persuaded to take another step in my life's journey.

In 1954, I travelled to Columbia, South Carolina with some friends made during the Summer. I had no aspirations for college even though the next step in my life occurred. I enrolled and became a student at Columbia Bible College (now called Columbia International University). It was at this institution that I learned the foundational principles of the Christian life, faith and practice. Godly and patient men invested their lives into the students so we could be better equipped to live the Christian life and to serve the Lord. The things I learned there have proven to be long-lasting in terms of my life and ministry.

I am especially grateful to different ones who influenced and impacted my life. Along the journey of educational preparation and ministry endeavor, they were of considerable encouragement. Most of these dear people are already in the presence of the Lord. As I write these words, my mind is flooded with memories of those who played an important role in my life. In a general way, this writing is dedicated to each of those mentioned. I am grateful to the Lord for each of them and their positive input for my family and me.. Some people would go unnoticed by the world and in the overall scheme of things but they fulfilled a purpose of God in and for my life.

As several are mentioned below, the words from a contemporary Christian song have meaning and application. The words were written by Ray Boltz. The lyrics address different ones the Lord used in one's life journey. The refrain throughout contains these words: "Thank you for giving to the Lord. I am a life that was changed. Thank you for giving to the Lord. I am so glad you gave." Some of those who gave and who changed my life for the better are:

Herbie Miller who was a friend and encourager. He took great pride in what the Lord was doing in my life. He was overjoyed when he learned I was going to a Bible College.

Mae Garrison, a poor African-American lady, who committed herself to pray for me every day. Every so often, sacrificially, she would send me $5.00 to help me in my schooling.

Mrs. Ilardi, a Roman Catholic lady, who lived in the same tenement where I was reared. When I would return home to visit my Mother, Mrs. Ilardi would tell me: "Every day I light a candle at church and pray for you."

Frank Grosshans, a godly man who knew the Bible thoroughly, would stop in my Office where we would have times of prayer together. Many times, the prayers were intense and we would be praying with tears. He would always close his prayer with these words: "Lord, help Jim to show neither fear nor favor toward man."

My Mother would always sign her notes and cards with the statement: "The Lord watch between me and thee while we are absent one from the other." She would occasionally include: "Be the best of whatever you are." My Mother lived long enough to be able to visit in some of the churches where I was privileged to serve.

There were several others (they know who they are) and if I listed them all their names it could easily become the source for another tome.

After completion of the college requirements, I enrolled in the recently formed Covenant Theological Seminary in St. Louis, Missouri. While there, I was influenced and trained by men who had come out of retirement to both found the institution and to train another generation of ministers. I am indebted to them for their kindness and helpfulness, as well as their scholarship. Their adherence to the Word of God and the fundamentals of the faith made an impact in my life. I am continually grateful for these men of sacrifice and principle who trained me well.

My hope and prayer is that I emulate both who and what all of these people were in my life. In a reciprocal way, I trust that I may have been able to be an influence for someone along the way. I give God the glory for entrusting me with that opportunity. The earlier mentioned song contains these words: "As Jesus took your hand and you stood before the Lord. He said: My child, look around you. Great is your reward."

"Whatever I am now, it is all because God poured out His special favor on me - and not without results," To God be all the glory for what He has done for and through me.

Preface

Many books have been written on the subject of The Culture and the various stages of it. One of the more recent, written by Erwin Lutzer, asked a question in its title: "Where Do We God From Here?" The opening words of the Preface to the book are very telling. Dr. Lutzer wrote: "It's gone. Some of you will remember when the Christian philosopher Francis Schaeffer told us back in the 1970s that someday we would wake up and find out that the America we once knew was gone. That day is here. We have crossed an invisible line, and there are no signs that we are capable of turning back. The "cultural war" we used to speak about appears to be over, and we have lost. Daily, perhaps hourly, we are losing the war for America's heart and mind."

A Promotional Statement about Bill O'Reilly's book, The Culture Warrior, is: "He sees that America is in the midst of a fierce culture war between those who embrace traditional values and those who want to change America into a "secular-progressive" country. This is a conflict that differs in many ways from the usual liberal/conservative divide, but it is no less heated, and the stakes are even higher."

Do you have a similar sense about the times in which we are currently living? Is the culture war over? Has it been fought and won by the anti-Christian influences around the world? Are the Social Progressives so entrenched around the world that cultural trends are irreversible? Is there any validity for the continuation of evangelism and missionary endeavor? Have we lost any possibility of hope and a better tomorrow? If so, what kind of meaning can we attach to Proverbs 29:18 (ASV), "Where there is no vision, the people cast off restraint; but he who keeps the law, happy is he."

The following pages will look at some of the trends that have become overwhelming and a strong influence upon the direction of the nation and world. Biblical History reminds us that there have been other times of major Cultural Captivities such as, the bondage in Egypt and The Babylonian Captivity. In these and other captivities, God proved His faithfulness and purpose as He delivered an indentured and oppressed people and gave them a new hope. A verse we would do well to keep in mind is Jeremiah 29:11 (NIV), "For I know the plans I have for you, declares the LORD, plans to prosper you and not to harm you, plans to give you hope and a future." He has done this before and we can be confident that He is capable of doing it again. May the Lord grant you challenge and encouragement as you read the following chapters.

Table of Contents

1. Scoping the Slope 1
2. What's in the Name 9
3. Who Am I? What is my Identity? 15
4. The Fork in the Road 23
5. Roadblocks on the Journey 29
6. Oil and Ice on the Slick Slope 37
7. A Learning Curve - Knowing God's Prerogatives 43
8. A Bent Bugle 49
9. Mind Renewal 55
10. What We Must Be 63
11. Being in the Arena 71
12. A Possession Perspective 77
13. A Stewardship Perspective 85
14. A Persecution Perspective 91
15. Getting the Gears to Mesh 99
16. Missing Ingredients 105
17. Misfits and Other Idiosyncrasies 113
18. Detriments and Impediments 119
19. Incalculable Imputations 127
20. Escape From Cultural Captivity 133

Final Word 141

1. Scoping the Slope

The times in which we live have seen many rapid transitions and ethical challenges. Moral and core values seem to have evaporated almost overnight. The 24-7 media appears to have the foothold in terms of mores and viewpoints. In the 1990s, Robert H. Bork, a former Federal Judge, published a book entitled: *Slouching Towards Gomorrah: Modern Liberalism and American Decline*. The focus of this tome included the areas of multiculturalism, racial realities, and sexual boundaries being removed. The Publishers Weekly was very negative toward Bork and his book. However, they shared this positive thought: "Bork does strike a chord with his criticisms that individualism and egalitarianism have loosened social ties and weakened America, and with his warnings that recent decisions on assisted suicide may have broad, Roe v. Wade-like implications."

While his views were shared forthrightly almost two decades ago, they were ignored and unheeded. His views were not a fit with the Politically Correct Agenda that was emerging and gaining a foothold. Earlier, Francis Schaeffer had put into writing some of his theological and philosophical perspective. He crystalized the Biblical worldview when he wrote: *A Christian Manifesto* more than 30 years ago. His basic thesis was: "Christian truth is not a truth of Sunday mornings. It is a truth about the God, man and the world as they are and a result has implications for how we pursue relationships, our basis for government, morals and every facet of human existence." He set out to deal with the application of Christian Truth across the broad spectrum of life. His narrower focus was in terms of how it related to government and social action. One can only wonder how these two men, Robert Bork and Francis Schaeffer, would react and respond to what is taking place in the culture and society today. The things about which they were sounding an alarm are the things that are rapidly occurring in this day. Additionally, one must ponder whether or not the culture, society and nation is already on the slippery slope and that the descent and decline has already begun. If that is the case, and it certainly appears that it is, the downward trend will gain momentum and increase the speed of the descent.

The church at large has begun to be more tolerant and accommodating regarding the behavioral trends that are different from Biblical virtue and standards. The church has lost some of its influence in the 21st century. The question is, why? Part of the decline is due to many events and experiences that are occurring at an accelerated rate. This leads to a culture, society and church that has become overwhelmed. When each area and entity is overwhelmed, other factors become buffers in terms of what is happening. It tends to dull awareness and allows for a sense and realization of the near- impossibility of being able to alter what is taking place. The chain of life begins to add links, such as: (a) being overwhelmed; (b) becoming indifferent (c) feeling lethargic; (d) resigning oneself to become acquiescent. When acquiescence occurs, the culture, society, church and individuals are found to passively "give tacit assent to that which is occurring; it is agreement or consent by silence or without objection; compliance." This posture and the life choices made contributes to the rise of false religions, cults, alternative lifestyles and consent to the least common denominator acceptance of things as they are in their varied forms. We are tolerating things in our culture and society such as the legalization of same gender unions; the legalization of marijuana use and a variety of other whims and/or unrestrained behavioral choices.

Other issues that can be attached to acquiescence are compromise and capitulation. The cultural pressures can become a dominant factor in terms of what one will either accept or oppose. To avoid conflict, too many acquiesce rather than becoming engaged in the discussion and debate regarding moral and core values versus cultural and societal trends and direction. For those who have expressed and embraced the Judeo-Christian lifestyle and values, some become engaged in a type of mental gymnastic in terms of how to adapt to that which is contrary to the long-held Judeo-Christian ethic. Some of this is due to the changing socioeconomic factors and values, as well as the cultural preferences that develop at particular historic points. A recent Opinion Column written by Larry Clayton, a professor of History at the University of Alabama, and published in the Tuscaloosa News on June 1, 2014 suggested the following: "Our culture and civilization change over time. What concerned people in this country in 1765 (leading up to independence from Great Britain) was different from 1865 (the end of the Civil War), and 1965…when women's liberation, the civil rights movement and the Vietnam War were all demanding our attention. As the Civil War drew to a close…a hot issue among Southerners was "why did we lose, and so catastrophically at that?" Whose side was God on in this immense internecine (marked by slaughter, mutually destructive) conflict that still casts shadows on our world today…?"

Clayton continues his thoughts when he writes: "Every age has to contend with the fact that while Scripture does not change, the customs, habits and culture of a civilization does change. The tough question…is how do we interpret Scripture when we have grown so complicated, so complex, so sophisticated, so modern, so scientific, so in-charge-of-it-all. Scripture seems, by contrast, to be static, antiquated, boring and old fashioned, and not relevant at all to the world in which we live. As the world tries to adapt Scripture to fit its own needs, the result is what theologians and scholars call the 'cultural captivity' of the Bible; or, how we adopt Biblical principles and rules and laws to our times. Or, put another way, each different culture of, let's say, the Roman Empire, or medieval Europe or of the Enlightenment reads and interprets Scripture to suit its fashions…" It is at this precise point where one would expect the church to give the clarion sound and enunciate the principles for life that are enduring. Has the church fulfilled its obligation and privilege? Regrettably, the trumpet of the church is giving an uncertain sound. On the landscape of the church one can find the elements of acquiescence, compromise and capitulation. It becomes easy to rationalize that it is a matter of survival versus extinction. The larger question is in terms of the focus of the church today. Is it committed to God's work being done in God's way regardless of the cost and risk, or is it concerned with what man thinks and how man will respond to the church that is adapting itself to the culture and society that is approaching the precipice of the slippery slope?

A Biblical passage that should be referenced states the encompassing worldview from God Himself as expressed in Isaiah 46:8-10 (ESV), "Remember this and stand firm, recall it to mind, you transgressors, remember the former things of old; for I am God, and there is no other; I am God, and there is none like me, declaring the end from the beginning and from ancient times things not yet done, saying: My counsel shall stand, and I will accomplish all my purpose," Any attempt by the church to finesse or adapt the word of God to the Cultural Trends will only result in God's frown and His shaking His head disapprovingly. Sin will always be sin before God; unrighteousness will never be modified by Him to make it seem to be righteous; the Gospel is uniform throughout all generations and cultural shifts, Sadly, the church is allowing for gradualism and a drift into a cultural captivity.

There has always been cultural and societal pressures. In some historical settings, the cultural and societal pressures were led by the religious community of the day. In Acts 4:1-21, there is a confrontation with the religious enforcers of the first century. After the ascension of Jesus Christ, the Apostles began to be engaged in the ministry Jesus Christ had assigned to them. They encountered a man with a physical need and healed him. This brought about the outcry and outrage of the religious community. Peter and John are arrested and placed in jail overnight. The next morning the question posed to them by the rulers, elders and scribes was (vs.7): "By what power or by what name did you do this?" At this point, the Apostles were not shy regarding their response. In verses 8-13 (ASV), Peter said: "You rulers of the people, and elders, if we this day are examined concerning a good deed done to an impotent man, by what means this man is made whole; be it known unto you all, and to all the people of Israel, that in the name of Jesus Christ of Nazareth, whom you crucified, whom God raised from the dead, in Him does this man stand here before you whole…And in none other is there salvation: for neither is there any other name under heaven, that is given among men, wherein we must be saved." Peter is giving an unequivocal response to a direct question. There is no fear of what man might do to him or the other Apostles. They did not acquiesce, compromise or capitulate. As a result, take note of what the leaders of the secular and religious community observed about them (verse 13): "Now when they beheld the boldness of Peter and John, and had perceived that they were unlearned and ignorant men, they marveled; and they took knowledge of them, that they had been with Jesus."

Also take note that the miracle occurred and the man was healed by the power and name of Jesus, the crucified, risen and ascended one. When the leaders observed the Apostles, they noted they were not of the elite or highly educated class, They had to concede that what made the difference in their lives and what they were doing had a singular focus and cause, namely, "…they took knowledge of them, that they had been with Jesus." There was one other observation they had to make because it was irrefutable and inescapable. The man they had healed was standing there with them. The leaders of that day conferred on what was the best way to handle this situation. Their plan was to threatened them with further consequences if they continually conducted their ministry. Their agreed upon action is given in verses 17-21: "…they called them, and charged them not to speak at all nor teach in the name of Jesus. But Peter and John answered and said unto them: "Whether it is right in the sight of God to hearken unto you rather than unto God, you judge: for we cannot but speak the things which we saw and heard. And they, when they had further threatened them, let them go, finding nothing how they might punish them, because of the people; for all men glorified God for that which was done."

How would you have responded to such challenges and threats? What would your response be to unjust incarceration? If you were told that you could freely go about your task providing that you never mentioned the name of Jesus, would you accept that condition? For far too many, they would acquiesce, compromise and/or capitulate. They would allow themselves to become cultural captives. The big question that should be pondered and answered is: What's in a name? What's the problem with proclaiming a focus and having a place for Jesus Christ within the culture and society? Lest you think this is a theoretical matter, an article appeared in the May 17, 2014 edition of World Magazine. The column has a focus on whether or not one can publicly pray in the name of Jesus. The column stated: "The Commissioners of Carroll County, MD., were doing fine until a few irate citizens noticed Robin Bartlett Frazier using "the name" in her pre-meeting prayers. They got the American Humanists Association to help them sue. Federal Judge William Quarles served an injunction, not forbidding prayer altogether, just forbidding "the name."

Notice the similarity between the first century declaration and the twenty-first century injunction. You can do your religious thing. Just don't use the name of Jesus or any inference of "the name" in public. The Maryland Court injunction is basically stating: (a) you can have your first amendment rights; (b) you can exercise your freedom of religion but you must stop using the name of Jesus; you must eliminate any reference or inference to things that are "Christian"; you must remove your displays, pictures, Christmas Carols, Easter Traditions etc., anything and everything that would be an influence on anyone in terms of Jesus only. The World Magazine article continued: "Ms. Frazier… explained to those in attendance the day after the March 26 ruling: 'There was an injunction…that came down that said, oh, we could pray, but we just can't use certain words, like 'Jesus,' and 'Lord,' and 'Savior.'…I think that's an infringement on my First Amendment rights of free speech. Also…I am willing to go to jail over it." Meanwhile, the "…plaintiffs sought contempt of court charges after county resident Bruce Holstein during public comment time invoked the name of Jesus. Frazier, for her part, desiring to show that the Founding Fathers were not averse to 'the name,' read a prayer found in a chest of George Washington's papers in the 1890s that contained the prosecutable phrase 'Jesus Christ.' Then began the dispute over authorship of Frazier's quoted prayer…"

Trending Toward Cultural Captivity

A dangerous path is before the Christian and the Church. If either acquiesce, compromise or capitulate, then the atheistic and anti-Christian agenda will find legitimacy. Just as in the first century, mere utterance of "the name" (except in profanity) will be grounds for censorship or having to give answer before the magistrate of the civil court. It will be almost immediate Cultural Captivity. In many ways, it would be similar to the Babylonian Captivity in 587 BC. The re-education and re-orientation was undertaken so the captives would learn the ways of their captors. Note the scope of what was taking place in Daniel 1:3-7. They were to "learn the literature and language of the Chaldeans; they were to eat the food that the king ate and drink the wine that the king drank; their intense education was to endure for three years, after which they would have to stand before the king for his inspection and approval; and then they would be given Chaldean names. In verses 6 and 7 we read, "...among these were Daniel, Hananiah, Mishael, and Azariah of the tribe of Judah. And the chief of the eunuchs gave them names: Daniel he called Belteshazzar, Hananiah he called Shadrach, Mishael he called Meshach, and Azariah he called Abednego."

There was one thing that no one in Babylon expected or anticipated. The commitment of these young men singled out for special attention and education was to the Lord Jehovah and they would not acquiesce, compromise or capitulate to the king's whims or wishes. Daniel is representative for the others and it is said of him in Daniel 1:8, "Daniel purposed in his heart that he would not defile himself with the king's dainties (food), nor with the wine which he drank." If you were a captive and your captors were endeavoring to change your way of thinking and that which you believe, what would you do? Would you go along outwardly to get along, or would you be bold and courageous and respectfully decline to participate in that which was contrary to your core principles and values? Would you be a conqueror or a casualty within the Cultural Captivity?

2. What's in the Name

The Culture acts as though it is obsessed as the effort is made to eliminate the name of Jesus and any other Christian inference from the American way of life. The American Civil Liberties Union (ACLU) regularly files court briefs in this regard. The Humanist and Atheist groups have been emboldened to make their positions known by any means possible. If they are successful in eliminating "the name" or any nuanced inferences to it from discourse within the human arena, then the Christian and Church will enter an entirely different phase for existence. We may have to endure rejection to the degree of those mentioned in Hebrews 11:35-38 (ASV), "…others were tortured, not accepting their deliverance; that they might obtain a better resurrection: and others had trials of mocking and scourging, yes, moreover of bonds and imprisonment: they were stoned, they were sawn asunder, they were tempted, they were slain with the sword: they went about in sheepskins, in goatskins; being destitute, afflicted, ill-treated (of whom the world was not worthy), wandering in deserts and mountains and caves, and the holes of the earth…" All of this because one's identity with "the name" that is above every name, The Name of Jesus. What's in that name and what should that mean to and for us?

Contemporary music has produced worship choruses that focus on The Name of Jesus. One of the choruses is: His Name Is Wonderful. The lyrics cover some of the basics regarding the names and ministry objective of Jesus Christ. Another worship chorus was written by Bill and Gloria Gaither and titled, There's Something About That Name. This chorus incorporates some of the titles Jesus bears and the impact that He had and will continue to have in the world. With this in mind, we will look at several names that are used in the Holy Scriptures to express Who God is and what God does/means. A few examples: (1) *Elohim*: Almighty, Strong, Creator; (2) *Jehovah*: He is present, accessible, near to those who call upon

Him for deliverance and help; (3) *Jehovah-Jireh*: The Lord will provide; (4) *Jehovah-Shalom*: The Lord is our peace; (5) *Jehovah-Rapha*: The Lord Who heals; (6) *Jehovah-rohi*: The Lord is my Shepherd; and (7) *Jehovah-Shammah*: The Lord is always there. When Moses was being designated by God to represent Him before the people and Pharaoh, Moses was apprehensive. His major concern was: "Why should the people listen to and or believe what I say to them?" His rationale could easily have been: I was raised in Pharoah's household and court. I was a Prince in Egypt and now the enslaved people will be expected to listen to me. I don't think so. Moses does pose this issue and question to the Lord: "Who shall I say sent me to you?" God's ready and immediate response appears in Exodus 3:11-15 (ASV): "And Moses said unto God, Who am I, that I should go unto Pharaoh, and that I should bring forth the children of Israel out of Egypt? And He said, Certainly I will be with you; and this shall be the token unto you, that I have sent you: when you have brought forth the people out of Egypt, you shall serve God upon this mountain. And Moses said unto God, Behold, when I come to the children of Israel, and shall say unto them: The God of your fathers hath sent me unto you; and they shall say to me, What is His name? What shall I say unto them? And God said unto Moses, I AM THAT I AM: and He said: This you shall say unto the children of Israel, I AM hath sent me unto you. And God said moreover unto Moses: This you shall say unto the children of Israel, Jehovah, the God of your fathers, the God of Abraham, the God of Isaac, and the God of Jacob, has sent me unto you: this is My name forever, and this is my memorial unto all generations."

In His earthly ministry, Jesus identified Himself with the "I AM" reality. It will represent the same words of hope and deliverance for the people He has come to seek and to save. In the Gospel of John, Jesus employed the "I AM' identity as He ministers in different need situations: (1) to those who were hungry, Jesus stated in John 6:48, "I AM the Bread of life"; (2) to those who were stumbling in the darkness of the world, Jesus stated in John 8:12, "I AM the Light of the world"; (3) to those who were vulnerable and/or disenfranchised, Jesus said in John 10:9, "I AM the Door, by

Me, if any man enters in, he will be saved"; (4) to those who were weak and an easy prey, Jesus stated in John 10:11, "I AM the Good Shepherd"; (5) to those who were sorrowful and mourning, Jesus stated in John 11:25, "I AM the Resurrection and the Life"; (6) to those who had been besieged by the various philosophies and heresies of the day, Jesus stated in John 14:6, "I AM the Way, the Truth and the Life, no one comes to the Father except by and through Me"; and (7) to those who can so easily be impacted by error and that which will cause harm, Jesus stated in John15:1, "I AM the vine, you are the branches…abide in Me that you may bear much fruit."

    The looming question of the day is in terms of how our culture and society will respond to the "I AM" and His requirement for our lives? Another soul-searching question is whether or not we will acquiesce, compromise or capitulate to the cultural and societal pressures of the day? If so, one will be numbered among the Cultural Captives. They will be useless and incapable of any valid kingdom work. Will we allow ourselves to be neutralized and silenced at a time when the message of truth needs to be proclaimed? It needs to be remembered that there is a day of reckoning approaching soon. The Apostle John wrote these words in Revelation 1:17-19 (ESV), "When I saw Him, I fell at his feet as though dead. But he laid his right hand on me, saying: Fear not, I am the first and the last, and the living one. I died, and behold I am alive forevermore, and I have the keys of Death and Hades."

    In that day, there will be the acknowledgement of Jesus Christ. The message that must be proclaimed courageously and with clarity is summarized in Isaiah 45:22-23 (ESV), "Turn to Me and be saved, all the ends of the earth! For I am God, and there is no other. By myself I have sworn; from My mouth has gone out in righteousness a word that shall not return: To Me every knee shall bow, every tongue shall swear allegiance." The thrust and clarity of The Lord's message is obvious. Thrust One: "Turn to Me." Throughout History, nations have reached a pinnacle when the culture departs from The Lord and His righteous ways. Carnality begins to gain a foothold and Spirituality becomes dormant. When

Jesus Christ ministered upon the earth, He employed a similar phrase to "Turn to Me." In Matthew 11:28-30, rather than saying "turn to Me", He states, "Come to Me…" He is appealing to "all who labor and are heavy laden…" His purpose is twofold: (1) "I will give you rest" and (2) "Take My yoke upon you, and learn from Me." What does He want those who come to Him to learn and know? His character and qualities available to the one who comes to Him are summarized in these words: "I AM gentle and lowly in heart, and you will find rest for your souls. For My yoke is easy, and my burden is light."

Thrust Two of the prophet's message: "Turn to Me and be saved, all the ends of the earth." This is similar to the thrust of Peter and John in Acts 4:12 (ESV), "And there is salvation in no one else, for there is no other name under heaven given among men by which we must be saved." The idea that there are many roads leading one to heaven is erroneous. The only way and road to God's Heaven is singular and narrow. The estimated population of the world in the twenty-first century is approximated to be seven billion people. Out of that seven billion, how many have turned to God and come to Jesus Christ for salvation and hope of eternal life in God's heaven? Would you think it is two-thirds of the world's population? What about the possibility of one-half? Could it be as many as one-fourth? Should we estimated it at less than one-seventh, maybe one billion people? This all sounds reminiscent to Abraham's plea in behalf of Sodom and Gomorrah. He inquired whether God would spare the cities if there were fifty righteous people in them. Abraham went through a subtraction process before the Lord until he had become convinced that God's impending judgment upon the wicked and sinful cities was just and right.

Thrust three of the prophet's message is: "Turn to Me…for I AM God and there is no other…" This declaration sets us on a collision course with multitudes of false religions and anti-Christian groups. Some of these groups are vindictive toward Jesus Christ, the Holy Scriptures and the proclamation of the Gospel. The question that must be asked and answered is: Are you willing to run the risk and echo the prophet's message from The Lord? Will you be vocal as His message is declared: "Turn to Me and be saved, all the ends of the earth, for I AM God and there is no other…?" Will you be a champion for this one true God?

The words of purpose and encouragement are summarized in The MSG paraphrase, Isaiah 45:23-24, "Everyone is going to end up kneeling before Me. Everyone is going to end up saying of Me: Yes! Salvation and strength are in God!" When the Apostle Paul reflected upon the sacrifice of Jesus Christ, he seems to have been unable to contain himself any longer when he wrote, Philippians 2:9-11, "God has highly exalted Him and bestowed on Him the name that is above every name, so that at the name of Jesus every knee should bow, in heaven and on earth and under the earth, and every tongue confess that Jesus Christ is Lord, to the glory of God the Father."

The Apostle John shares this scene from heaven in Revelation 4:11. It takes place at the throne of God where the faithful followers and servants of Jesus Christ will witness and share in the song and expression of worship: "Worthy are you, our Lord and God, to receive glory and honor and power, for You created all things, and by Your will they existed and were created." This is the moment of completeness and finality for those whose chief end was to glorify God and enjoy Him forever. This is that moment of perfect fulfillment and realization. We have been delivered from Cultural Captivity by Him Who alone is worthy to receive glory and honor and power. Worthy is The Lamb Who was slain. To God be all the glory for the great things He alone has done.

Regardless of the pressures from those who advocate Cultural Captivity, the Christian and the Church should stand solidly on the foundation Jesus Christ. The message must go forth as a trumpet call for battle. The response to the clarion call must be immediate. There is no time to waste and any delay will allow for Cultural Captivity types to gain an advantage and foothold. We need to identify with Polycarp of the First Century (who refused to recant as he was being burned at the stake) and Martin Luther of the

Sixteenth Century (as he faced unknown dangers) stated: "Here I stand, I can do no other, so help me God."

3. Who Am I? What is my Identity?

The Book of Acts shares not only the History of the early church but also the transitioning of it from a near-exclusive Jewish frame of reference to a more inclusive one as the Gentiles were being received into the ongoing ministry of the church. It begins in Acts 10 as Peter has a vision of a more inclusive ministry that would stretch him beyond his comfort zone. He would have to go to the home of Cornelius (a Gentile) and minister there in Christ's name. Even though there was an element of protest and reluctance by Peter, he obediently did that which the Lord was directing him to do.

Acts 11 tells of the stirring and moving of the hearts of many in Antioch, When Barnabas observed all that the Lord is doing, he left to seek out Saul in Tarsus. Acts 11:25-26 (ASV) records: "So Barnabas went to Tarsus to look for Saul, and when he had found him, he brought him to Antioch. For a whole year they met with the church and taught a great many people. And in Antioch the disciples were first called Christians." The statement that stands out is "the disciples were first called Christians" in Antioch. The name "Christian" is comparatively rare. It appears three times in the New Testament (1) Acts 11:26, (2) Acts 26:28 as Paul stands before King Agrippa who stated to Paul: "In a short time would you persuade me to be a Christian?" and (3) I Peter 4:16 (NKJV)."Yet if anyone suffers as a Christian, let him not be ashamed, but let him glorify God in this matter."

Paul and Peter both share an interesting concept in their travels and ministries. Paul uses a different idea when he writes to the Church at Ephesus (Ephesians 3:4). "In reading this, then, you will be able to understand my insight into the mystery of Christ." In a similar way, Paul mentions in Colossians 4:3, "And pray for us, too, that God may open a door for our message, so that we may proclaim the mystery of Christ, for which I am in chains." In his trying to understand more of the meaning of Paul's words regarding "the mystery of Christ" Peter would write to the believers who were being scattered because of the persecution by Rome, II Peter 3:15-16, "Bear in mind that our Lord's patience means salvation, just as our dear brother Paul also wrote you with the wisdom that God gave him. He writes the same way in all his letters, speaking in them of these matters. His letters contain some things that are hard to understand, which ignorant and unstable people distort, as they do the other Scriptures, to their own destruction." Peter was acknowledging what Paul referred to as "my insight into the mystery of Christ." He also states that Paul's letters contain some things that are hard to understand! It is possible that Peter wrote this statement because of the tension he was experiencing between Judaism and the Jewish Culture with this emerging ministry with the Hellenistic and Grecian Culture. Many times, there is some tension and difficulty when adapting and adjusting is a necessity.

Paul would make it a point to indicate clearly to the churches with which he had contact and ministry what it meant to be a follower of Jesus Christ. One passage making this point abundantly clear is II Corinthians 5:15-21 (ASV) where Paul wrote: "For the love of Christ constrains us…and he died for all, that they that live should no longer live unto themselves, but unto him who for their sakes died and rose again…Wherefore if any man is in Christ, he is a new creature: the old things are passed away; behold, they are become new. But all things are of God, who reconciled us to himself through Christ, and gave unto us the ministry of reconciliation…We are ambassadors therefore on behalf of Christ, as though God were entreating by us, we beseech you on behalf of Christ, be ye reconciled to God. Him who knew no sin he made to be sin on our behalf; that we might become the righteousness of God in him."

The questions of this chapter are: (1) Who am I? and (2) What is my identity? The answer is stated in the above passage. Question 1 asks: Who am I? The answer is verse 17: "if any man is in Christ, he is a new creature: the old things are passed away; behold, they are become new." The MSG paraphrase is: "Now we look inside, and what we see is that anyone united with the Messiah gets a fresh start, is created new. The old life is gone; a new life burgeons!" This is the product of God's love and the work of God's grace. Before God, no one is able to claim to be a self-made man or woman. God knows better than that and we should too. Question 2 asks: What is my identity? The answer is: I am a "new creature" (or creation) in Jesus Christ. It is a life in which there is a process operating within one as the old things pass away and all things are becoming new. It becomes a life where (Vs. 15), "those who live no longer live unto themselves but unto Him Who died for them and rose again."

This process is not something that happens immediately. It begins in the here and now but there is a work that has begun. In a theological term, it is known as sanctification. The basic explanation of sanctification is that; "it is the work of God's free grace, whereby we are renewed in the whole man after the image of God, and are enabled more and more to die unto sin, and live unto righteousness." The Scriptures that substantiate this definition are: (1) II Thessalonians 2:13-14 (ASV), "God chose you from the beginning unto salvation in sanctification of the Spirit and belief of the truth: whereunto he called you through our gospel, to the obtaining of the glory of our Lord Jesus Christ." (2) Ephesians 4:23-24, "Be renewed in the spirit of your mind, and put on the new man, that after God hath been created in righteousness and holiness of truth." (3) Romans 6:6-14, "knowing this, that our old man was crucified with Him, that the body of sin might be done away, that so we should no longer be in bondage to sin…For sin shall not have dominion over you: for you are not under law, but under grace." Romans 8:1-5 is an excellent statement that addresses both questions concerning (a) Who am I? and (b) What is my identity? Paul wrote: "There is therefore now no condemnation to them who are in Christ Jesus. For the law of the Spirit of life in Christ Jesus made me free from the law of sin and of death. For what the law could not do, in that it was weak through the flesh, God, sending his own Son in the likeness of sinful flesh and for sin, condemned sin in the flesh, that the ordinance of the law might be fulfilled in us, who walk not after the flesh, but after the Spirit. For they that are after the flesh mind the things of the flesh; but they that are after the Spirit the things of the Spirit."

Prior to one being in Christ and becoming a new creation, there was no conscious awareness of the spiritual struggle that would ensue. The old things passing away and all things becoming new is not a process that occurs by osmosis (an ability to learn and understand things gradually without much effort). Everything stated in Scripture regarding the new life in Christ references that there is an element of struggle involved in this process. It will require both discipline and perseverance as the process unfolds. One illustration of this is given in Galatians 5 where the contrast between the lust of the flesh versus the fruit of the spirit is clearly given. The possibility and potential of victory in this area is also clearly given. The life lived that caters to the lust of the flesh is a life of bondage and cultural captivity. The life that pursues walking in the Spirit is one that knows the benefit of both freedom and victory in the Lord Jesus Christ. Galatians 5:13-26 is the all-encompassing passage dealing with the contrasts and conflicts between the flesh and the spirit.

The basic premise of this section is stated in verse 13, "you were called for freedom; only do not use your freedom for an occasion to the flesh." What a joyous sound in the words, "you were called for freedom." It is a freedom that is no longer self-seeking but one that endeavors to be God-pleasing. The path that enables one to enter and journey in that reality is given in verse 16, "walk by the Spirit, and you shall not fulfill the lust of the flesh." The meaning of the phrase, "walk by the Spirit", if it was translated literally would read: "walk by the enablement of the Spirit." This new life in Christ and the growth in spiritual things is not a solo flight. We cannot achieve the basic requirements or desired result independently. It can and will only be accomplished by the enabling ministry of the Holy Spirit.

Jesus instructed His disciples about the scope of ministry that would be done by the Comforter (Holy Spirit) after the ascension of Jesus Christ into heaven. In John 16:7-15, the particular areas the Holy Spirit will address are indicated. "And He, when He is come, will convict the world in respect of sin, and of righteousness, and of judgment: of sin, because they believe not on Me; of righteousness, because I go to the Father, and you behold me no more; of judgment, because the prince of this world has been judged…when He, the Spirit of truth, is come, He shall guide you into all the truth…He shall glorify me…" The multiple task of the Holy Spirit in our individual and personal lives will concentrate on four areas: (1) convict us regarding sin; (2) convict us regarding righteousness; (3) convict us regarding the reality of judgment and (4) guide us into all the truth. Why is this so vital and necessary for us in the pathway of becoming the new creatures God desires us to be?

The necessity for the Holy Spirit's presence in our lives is due to our need for a a Guide Who will lead us through the mine field of fleshly enticements and temptations. He will enable us to differentiate between that which is right and best for us. He will enable us to know the precise choice that is safest and wisest for us. Galatians 5:17 indicates the lines of battle as we journey through life: "the flesh lusts against the Spirit, and the Spirit against the flesh; for these are contrary the one to the other." Verse 19 is a partial catalog of the works of the flesh. The verse indicates that these are some of things that are "manifest": fornication, uncleanness, lasciviousness, idolatry, sorcery, enmities, strife, jealousies, wraths, factions, divisions, parties, envying, drunkenness, reveling, and such like." The "such like" things are suggested in the MSG paraphrase of verses 19-21 is: "It is obvious what kind of life develops out of trying to get your own way all the time: repetitive, loveless, cheap sex; a stinking accumulation of mental and emotional garbage; frenzied and joyless grabs for happiness; trinket gods; magic-show religion; paranoid loneliness; cutthroat competition; all-consuming-yet-never-satisfied wants; a brutal temper; an impotence to love or be loved; divided homes and divided lives; small-minded and lopsided pursuits; the vicious habit of depersonalizing everyone into a rival; uncontrolled and uncontrollable addictions; ugly parodies of community. I could go on." The importance and seriousness of these matters is seen in the words of verse 21, "of which I forewarn you...that they who practice such things shall not inherit the kingdom of God." This all boils down to whether or not one is taking a serious God seriously. If so, the pathway that so many take leading to cultural captivity will be repugnant to you.

The positive contrast to the lust of the flesh is outlined in verses 22-23, "But the fruit of the Spirit is love, joy, peace, long-suffering, kindness, goodness, faithfulness, meekness, self-control; against such there is no law." This reminds one of the words of Jesus Christ in John 15:4-5, "Abide in Me, and I in you. As the branch cannot bear fruit of itself, except it abide in the vine; so neither can you, except you abide in Me. I am the vine, you are the branches: He that abides in Me, and I in him, the same bears much fruit: for apart from Me you can do nothing." Two other fruit of the Spirit are touched upon in John 15:10-11, "If ye keep My commandments, you shall abide in My love; even as I have kept My Father's commandments, and abide in His love. These things have I spoken unto you, that My joy may be in you, and that your joy may be made full."

The identity and testimony of the follower of Jesus Christ is unique because one has both an obligation and privilege in a particular way: "they that are in Christ Jesus have crucified the flesh with the passions and the lusts thereof. If we live by the Spirit, by the Spirit let us also walk. Let us not become vainglorious, provoking one another, envying one another." A final thought: Do you know who you are? If you have received Jesus Christ as your Savior and Lord, you are a new creature in Jesus Christ who has been redeemed by His blood and reconciled with God. Do you know what your identity is? If you have committed your life to Jesus Christ and are committed to do His will, you are a spiritual being who has the presence of the Holy Spirit in you Who is enabling you to walk in the right pathway and to make wise choices for your life. The one who refuses to go in the direction of the Holy Spirit's guidance is running the risk of both grieving the Holy Spirit of God and quenching the Spirit. The Spirit wants one to know the reality of His personalized ministry for and in each of us who believes and obeys. Do you have and know this relationship? It reminds one of the words in an old Hymn: "Trust and obey, for there's no other way."

4. The Fork in the Road

A statement that was allegedly made by the baseball player, Yogi Berra, was: "When you come to a fork in the road, take it!" While he may have meant that to be humorous, there is a very sobering thought and ultimate consequence if one has made the wrong decision and choice. The focus of this chapter is in terms of making a decision between which road one will travel. Will it be a secular road or a spiritual one? Will it be a choice between the desires of the flesh or the enabling control of the Holy Spirit? In I Corinthians 3:1-3, Paul raises this question: "I...could not speak unto you as unto spiritual, but as unto carnal, as unto babes in Christ. I fed you with milk, not with meat; for you were not yet able to bear it: no, not even now are you able; for you are yet carnal: for whereas there is among you jealousy and strife, are you not carnal, and do you not walk after the manner of men?"

The Dictionary definition of carnal is very succinct. Carnal: "pertains to or is characterized by the flesh or the body, its passions and appetites; the sensual," When amplified, it indicates that Carnal Pleasures are those things that are: "not spiritual; but merely human; temporal; and worldly." A Biblical description of this condition is given in Romans 8:5-9, "For they that are after the flesh mind the things of the flesh; but they that are after the Spirit the things of the Spirit. For the mind of the flesh is death; but the mind of the Spirit is life and peace: because the mind of the flesh is enmity against God; for it is not subject to the law of God, neither indeed can it be: and they that are in the flesh cannot please God. But you are not in the flesh but in the Spirit, if so be that the Spirit of God dwells in you. But if any man hath not the Spirit of Christ, he is none of his." These verses clearly define the different roads and choices one will make in life. One fork of the road will seek to satisfy the flesh and influences of the world. The other fork of the road will seek after the things of God, the fruit of the Spirit and that which will glorify and honor God in one's life.

Paul addresses this conflict between the things of the flesh versus the things of the Spirit when he writes in Galatians 6:7-8, "Be not deceived; God is not mocked: for whatever a man sows, that shall he also reap. For he who sows unto his own flesh shall of the flesh reap corruption; but he that sows unto the Spirit shall of the Spirit reap eternal life." Paul is wanting the followers of Christ to understand that the distinction between walking according to the flesh and walking according to Spirit is no trifling matter. The words: "Be not deceived: God is not mocked" should be etched in each one's heart and soul, as well as indelibly written within each one's conscience and mind. One must not trifle with God.

James is very blunt and clear when he writes about the factions between and among people. He uses terms such as wars and fightings. He indicates that this spirit of rivalry and contention is driven by individual fleshly desires. In James 4:2-4, he continues: "You lust, and have not: you kill, and covet, and cannot obtain: you fight and war; you have not, because you ask not. You ask, and receive not, because you ask amiss, that you may spend it in your pleasures. You adulteresses, know you not that the friendship of the world is enmity with God? Whosoever therefore would be a friend of the world makes himself an enemy of God." James is concerned about the disconnect between the values people have claimed to embrace and the lifestyle choices and actions that deny those values. He is concerned about their lives being lived in contradiction to the verities of God. One must always be guarded against allowing for complicity, compromise and acquiescence to influence life's values and choices.

An article by Billy Graham was released in September 2010 that expands on these choices by going a step further when he asks: "Are you a Carnal Christian? Does that describe you? If so, would you like to change? There was a time, perhaps, when you were a spiritual Christian. You still had your first love; a fire burned in your heart for God. But something has happened along the way, something has disturbed your relationship with God, and you no longer know the joy, the peace and the thrill that you once knew…" One of the things that can cause this spiritual shift to occur is the tendency to confuse religious activity with spiritual relationship. One begins to think that busyness in church related activities and religious studies equates with an established relationship to Jesus Christ. Just a quick read of Revelation 2 and 3 would serve to instruct one otherwise. The seven churches reviewed and assessed by Jesus Christ were busy in their church related activities. Most of them were noted for the stand they had taken against the evil present in that day and the false teaching that had been promulgated. Jesus stated emphatically that religious identity was insufficient and inadequate. The requirement and necessity was a spiritual relationship and loyalty to Jesus Christ alone. Carnal will never be an acceptable substitute for the Spiritual.

A question that should be pondered and answered is: Can a person fashioned after the heart of God do things that are contrary to the directive will of God? In this regard, a contemplative study should be done of Romans 6, 7 and 8. Paul is very transparent about the life one is supposed to live and those things which drag one away from that lifestyle. He wrote in Romans 6:8-14, "...knowing this, that our old man was crucified with Him, that the body of sin might be done away, so that we should no longer be in bondage to sin; for he that has died is justified from sin. But if we died with Christ, we believe that we shall also live with Him; knowing that Christ being raised from the dead dies no more; death no more has dominion over Him. For the death that He died, He died unto sin once: but the life that He lives, He lives unto God. Even so you should reckon yourselves to be dead unto sin, but alive unto God in Christ Jesus. Let not sin therefore reign in your mortal body, that ye should obey the lusts thereof: neither present your members unto sin as instruments of unrighteousness; but present yourselves unto God, as alive from the dead, and your members as instruments of righteousness unto God. For sin shall not have dominion over you: for you are not under law, but under grace." Paul is declaring how one's life is supposed to be lived. It is the ideal of a fully consecrated and obedient life in Christ.

Paul is also clear and realistic in terms of one's human nature. An ongoing conflict takes place in the heart and mind about that which is right and honoring to God and that which is wrong and dishonoring to Him. Paul wrote about this in as transparent way possible in Romans 7:14-25. Note the words he employs to describe this inner conflict, "For we know that the law is spiritual: but I am carnal, sold under sin…But if what I would not, that I do, I consent unto the law that it is good. So now it is no more I that do it, but sin which dwells in me. For I know that in me, that is, in my flesh, dwells no good thing: for to will is present with me, but to do that which is good is not. For the good which I would I do not: but the evil which I would not, that I practice. But if what I would not, that I do, it is no more I that do it, but sin which dwells in me. I find then the law, that, to me who would do good, evil is present. For I delight in the law of God after the inward man: but I see a different law in my members, warring against the law of my mind, and bringing me into captivity under the law of sin which is in my members. Wretched man that I am! who shall deliver me out of the body of this death? I thank God through Jesus Christ our Lord. So then I of myself with the mind, indeed, serve the law of God; but with the flesh the law of sin." His terms of transparency include:

- I am carnal, sold under sin
- The things I hate are the things I do
- In my flesh dwells no good thing
- To will is present with me
- Evil is present
- I see a different law warring against the law of my mind
- It brings me into captivity under the law of sin
- Wretched man that I am who shall deliver me out of the body of this death
- I serve the law of sin

Paul has to work through an intense area which he refers to as: "It brings me into captivity." It lends itself to the societal trends and cultural captivity of our day. Paul's resounding personal hope and the encouraging word for those with similar struggles is that deliverance is in Jesus Christ alone: "I thank God through Jesus Christ the Lord." He also addresses one further aspect of this conflict between the flesh and spirit in Romans 8:1-10, "There is therefore now no condemnation to them that are in Christ Jesus. For the law of the Spirit of life in Christ Jesus made me free from the law of sin and of death…For they that are after the flesh mind the things of the flesh; but they that are after the Spirit the things of the Spirit. For the mind of the flesh is death; but the mind of the Spirit is life and peace…But ye are not in the flesh but in the Spirit, if so be that the Spirit of God dwells in you. But if any man hath not the Spirit of Christ, he is none of his. And if Christ is in you, the body is dead because of sin; but the spirit is life because of righteousness."

The conclusion of this in Romans 8 is pregnant with hope and the new reality for the one who is in Jesus Christ. The words of Verses 35-39 include: "Who shall separate us from the love of Christ? Shall tribulation, or anguish, or persecution, or famine, or nakedness, or peril, or sword? …No, in all these things we are more than conquerors through him that loved us…(Nothing) shall be able to separate us from the love of God, which is in Christ Jesus our Lord." An older Hymn that was written more than sixty years ago makes an emphatic statement: "My Hope Is In The Lord, Who gave Himself for me…" This truth can be and should be the theme of your life and the confidence you have in Jesus Christ. Is that your hope today?

When one comes to the fork in the road and makes a choice, if the road of carnality and the flesh is chosen, it will result in misery and death; if the road of righteousness and spiritual fruit is chosen, the result will be fullness of joy and complete victory in Jesus Christ. The only way to be free from the Trend Toward Cultural Captivity is to choose and walk on the path of righteousness. You will never be alone on this road because Jesus Christ will be your constant companion and the Holy Spirit will guide you into all truth. Be encouraged and emboldened as you face each new day!

5. Roadblocks on the Journey

When one begins the spiritual journey, different hindrances and roadblocks can occur that prevent one's desired goal and progress. Departure from or modification of God's Truth in the Word of God is the greatest cause of hindrance in one's life in particular and society's in general. It is the beginning point of one entering into Cultural Captivity. The previous Chapter discussed the battle between the flesh and the Spirit. What constitutes a carnal lifestyle and that which differentiates it from a spiritual lifestyle? If someone presented to you suggestions regarding the battle between the mind of the flesh and the mind of the Spirit, what do you think those suggestions would include?

There is a real and present danger in resorting to the Internet for answers to life's questions and needs. With the subject of the spiritual conflict and what in entails, one proposition put forth is titled: "The Five Mental Hindrances and Their Conquest." Many people could easily be enticed by that assertion. The article states: "Many are the obstacles which block the road to spiritual progress, but there are five in particular which, under the name of hindrances…are often mentioned: (1) Sensual desire, (2) Ill-will, (3) Sloth and torpor (sluggish inactivity), (4) Restlessness and remorse, and (5) Skeptical doubt…They are called hindrances because they hinder and envelop the mind in many ways, obstructing its development." Does this resonate with you? Do you identify with the concept? What is the source for these postulates? What is the origin of these thoughts and ideas? The answer is: They originate and come from Buddha's doctrine. Just because something sounds good does not mean that it is good. One should endeavor to exercise discernment in the teaching that is heard, read, or embraced.

This needs to be noted because Jesus cautioned about one's susceptibility to such things when He stated in the Olivet Discourse, Matthew 24:24-25, "For there shall arise false christs, and false prophets, and shall show great signs and wonders; so as to lead astray, if possible, even the elect. Behold, I have told you beforehand." Paul reiterated these thoughts in II Thessalonians 2:8-12, "And then shall be revealed the lawless one, whom the Lord Jesus shall slay with the breath of his mouth, and bring to nought by the manifestation of his coming; even he, whose coming is according to the working of Satan with all power and signs and lying wonders, and with all deceit of unrighteousness for them that perish; because they received not the love of the truth, that they might be saved. And for this cause God sends them a working of error (a strong delusion), that they should believe a lie: that they all might be judged who believed not the truth, but had pleasure in unrighteousness."

When dealing with the matters of the heart and soul and mind, it can become easy to turn onto a road that will become impassable. There may be potholes or sinkholes; obstacles or obstructions; unknown dangers and risks that await one. This is true as one tries to arrive at a determination whether or not one is carnal or spiritual. Saying that such determinations can be difficult is an understatement. Mental wrestling in terms of what is or isn't carnal or what is or isn't spiritual is not unusual nor should it be unexpected. Our lives are filled with complexity and decisions need to be made soundly.

One gnawing consideration is whether or not a believer in the Lord Jesus Christ can continue as a carnal Christian. Can one vacillate between being a "spiritual Christian" and being a "carnal Christian"? Can one straddle the Biblical and spiritual fence with such an important and basic matter? Is this a possibility or an anomaly? The previously mentioned article by Billy Graham that was released in September 2010 asked: "Are you a Carnal Christian? Does that describe you? If so, would you like to change?" The question contains and makes an assumption that a Christian can be either a spiritual or carnal Christian. The Graham article continues: "There was a time, perhaps, when you were a spiritual Christian. You still had your first love; a fire burned in your heart for God. But something has happened along the way, something has disturbed your relationship with God, and you no longer know the joy, the peace and the thrill that you once knew." At this point, one must examine where one is positionally and relationally. According to John 15:10-11, Jesus said: "If you keep my commandments, you shall abide in my love; even as I have kept my Father's commandments, and abide in his love. These things have I spoken unto you, that my joy may be in you, and that your joy may be made full." The joy one should have continually results from a relationship that entails abiding and obeying. The same would be true with peace. Jesus stated in John 14:27, "Peace I leave with you; my peace I give unto you: not as the world giveth, give I unto you. Let not your heart be troubled, neither let it be fearful." Jesus has left us a legacy of peace in Him. He has also offered His gift of peace as a constant benefit for us. This peace comes from an established and maintained relationship with Jesus Christ.

The Graham article continues with temporal factors that can be construed as carnal: "You do not take time to read your Bible. Your prayer times are few. Your interest in spiritual things has waned..." These are factors that indicate a coldness or lukewarmness toward the things of God. It can be a disinterest or a failure of a disciplined life that causes a distance toward spiritual things to develop. As the Graham article continues, there is a touching of a spiritual nerve when he notes: "and yet there is a great hungering after God, an aching in your soul for the joy and victory that you have seen in the lives of others. You want that joy in your soul, that thrill in your heart. You want to know the power of prayer again." This can be true based upon a reality for all mankind. What is that reality? In Ecclesiastes 3:11 and 14 (NKJV), we read: "He has made everything beautiful in its time. Also He has put eternity in their hearts...I know that whatever God does, It shall be forever. Nothing can be added to it, And nothing taken from it. God does it, that men should fear before Him." The longing deep within the soul of an individual is for satisfaction and fulfillment. Deep within one's heart and soul, there is an itch caused by a desire for meaning and permanence. It can only be scratched by the Holy Spirit as He applies God's Word to the hungry, needy soul and as He fills the empty heart with eternity's values. As a young man, a popular chorus sung at Bible Conferences contained these words: "With eternity's values in view, Lord; with eternity's values in view; may I do each day's work for Jesus, with eternity's values in view." Is a value and choice in your life?

In thinking further about the dichotomy between being a carnal or spiritual Christian, a question that should be considered is in the area of a false start. Did a person go through the motion of becoming a spiritual Christian when in fact there was no conviction of sin or repentance? Was it well-intentioned? Did this person respond to the Gospel message out of a moment of emotion or because of the Holy Spirit's intervention in one's heart, soul and mind? Did that intervention result in conviction of sin and unrighteousness? Did it lead to one becoming a new creature in Jesus Christ? The Graham response continues: "From the divine viewpoint, defeated Christians are abnormal. They are paralyzed members of the Body of Christ. Backsliding and carnality are not only inexcusable, they are incompatible with the normal Christian experience. They produce a regime of contradiction. Since the living Christ dwells within every one who has received Him as Savior, there is never any reason for defeat. No enemy is too powerful for Christ! Every temptation may be resisted! If you as a Christian are overcome by the enemy, the simple explanation is that Christ has been denied His rightful position of supremacy in your heart. The dethronement of Christ will always lead to failure in spiritual warfare. It is Christ, and Christ alone, who can give you a constant, daily, victorious life." One's life can be and needs to be lived in Christ alone. The benefit and result will be the realization of His victory in us and for us.

The concern about whether one is a carnal or a spiritual Christian takes on added meaning and significance when Jesus said in the sermon on the Mount, Matthew 7:18-23, "A good tree cannot bring forth evil fruit, neither can a corrupt tree bring forth good fruit. Every tree that brings not forth good fruit is hewn down, and cast into the fire. Therefore by their fruits ye shall know them. Not every one that saith unto me, 'Lord, Lord,' shall enter into the kingdom of heaven; but he that does the will of my Father who is in heaven. Many will say to me in that day, 'Lord, Lord,' did we not prophesy by Thy name, and by Thy name cast out demons, and by Thy name do many mighty works? And then will I profess unto them, I never knew you: depart from me, you that work iniquity." Jesus had said earlier in this sermon, Matthew 7:13-14 (NKJV), "Enter by the narrow gate; for wide is the gate and broad is the way that leads to destruction, and there are many who go in by it. Because narrow is the gate and difficult is the way which leads to life, and there are few who find it." All of these words of Jesus is in a context of "by their fruit you will know them." If a life exhibits the fruit of the flesh (carnal), it is in danger of being on the wrong road beset with roadblocks. It will only lead to separation from Jesus Christ and prevention of being on the narrow way that leads to life evermore. If a life exhibits the fruit of the Spirit (spiritual), that one is abiding in Christ and will know the reality of being with Him for eternity.

All of this echoes what John wrote in his epistles. I John 5:10-13 (NKJV) is as clear and plain as the Gospel message can be. He wrote: "He who believes in the Son of God has the witness in himself; he who does not believe God has made Him a liar, because he has not believed the testimony that God has given of His Son. And this is the testimony: that God has given us eternal life, and this life is in His Son. He who has the Son has life; he who does not have the Son of God does not have life. These things I have written to you who believe in the name of the Son of God, that you may know that you have eternal life, and that you may continue to believe in the name of the Son of God."

Many years ago a pamphlet was written entitled: Roadblocks Limiting Church Effectiveness by J. G. Vos. The first roadblock he discussed was departure from The Truth. It is an obvious starting point because Jesus indicated in John 8:32, "And you shall know the truth, and the truth shall make you free." He would emphasize this once again in John 14:6 where he said: "I am the way, the truth, and the life. No one comes to the Father except through Me." A sermon was preached on this verse where the point was made several times,

"Jesus said I AM the way, I AM the life, and that is the Absolute Truth." Since He is The Truth, any variance from Him is a form of denial of Him and His character.

In 1919, Benjamin M. Ramsey wrote the Hymn, Teach Me Thy Way. One of the Stanzas contains the lyric, "When doubts and fears arise, teach me Thy way! When clouds o'er spread the skies, teach me Thy way…" In John 1:14, the words are very compelling: "The Word became flesh, and dwelt among us and we beheld his glory, glory as of the only begotten from the Father, full of grace and truth." Jesus Christ became the personification of both Grace and Truth as He lived upon this earth and among mankind. It is this undeniable truth that one must embrace and to which one must adhere.

There is always an occasion for pause when one begins to drift away from spiritual verities and to allow for carnality to creep in. The Scriptures remind us of the peril when this begins to occur. II Thessalonians 2:11-12 (NKJV), "And for this reason God will send them strong delusion, that they should believe the lie, that they all may be condemned who did not believe the truth but had pleasure in unrighteousness." The crux of the issue stated here is that they (1) "did not believe the truth" and they began to have (2) "pleasure in unrighteousness." It is couched in a vital phrase "that they should believe the lie." The lie can include something that sounds innocuous, such as, one can dabble in a little bit of sin and be unaffected spiritually. That kind of rationale flies in the face of Psalm 1:1-2 (NKJV), "Blessed is the man who walks not in the counsel of the ungodly, nor stands in the path of sinners, nor sits in the seat of the scornful; but his delight is in the law of the Lord, and in His law he meditates day and night." The progression of innocuous sin becomes obvious. The first step is: Walking in the pathway of sinners. The second step is: Standing in the pathway of sinners (suggesting a longing for and gazing at that which is inappropriate). The third step is: Sitting in the seat of the scorners (being comfortable in an association and camaraderie with those who have an apathy or denial toward spiritual truths). Another aspect to this is stated in Hebrews 4:2 (NKJV), "For indeed the gospel was preached to us as well as to them; but the word which they heard did not profit them, not being mixed with faith in those who heard it." An attempt to make a category of Carnality that can be acceptable is ignoring the phrase "but the word which they heard did not profit them, not being mixed with faith in those who heard it." The absence of faith is crucial in understanding the distinction made in Scripture between the one who has everlasting life and the one who does not have it.

Little things, those that one might consider insignificant, can very easily become very vital and large considerations before God. To grant one the benefit of the doubt in terms of being a spiritual or a carnal follower of Jesus Christ is correct in terms of the final judgment of Jesus Christ with such an individual. We need to be guarded that the one who doubts should be granted the benefit of being endorsed by us as being a true follower of Jesus Christ. There has to be the use of common sense and fair evaluations. We should never allow ourselves to condone that which God has clearly condemned. An expression that was sometimes used is: "We are not to be judges lest we be judged but that doesn't mean we're not supposed to be fruit inspectors."

A retired Baptist Minister on Facebook includes his Journal comments and other pithy thoughts. One of them was based on Job 4:4, "Your words have stood men on their feet." His devotional began with the theme: "It's Such a Little Thing." He tells the following story: "A pastor in Haiti tells about a fellow he knew who wanted to sell his house for $2,000. In time, he found a buyer, but the man could scrape together only half the asking price. The owner agreed to sell for that amount but with one reservation: he would continue to own one nail above the front door. A couple of years later, the first fellow decided he wanted to repurchase the house. The new owner declined, saying, 'I like this house; I don't want to sell.' The previous owner found the carcass of a dead dog on the street and hung it from the nail he still owned above the front door. Soon the stench became so strong no one could go in or out of the house, and the family had to leave. They sold the house to the former owner. The Haitian pastor said: If we leave the devil with even one small peg in our life, he will return to hang his rotting garbage on it, making our lives unfit for Christ's habitation." This truth applies to all who would seek to straddle the fence and attempt to have one foot in the flesh and the other in the Spirit. It is foolish to conceive of such a thing and far more foolish to think one can live this way.

The questions of II Corinthians 6:15-16 (ESV) must never be ignored or forgotten: "What portion does a believer share with an unbeliever? What agreement has the temple of God with idols?" A similar question is raised in Amos 3:3 (MSG), "Do two people walk hand in hand if they aren't going to the same place?" Going down the Carnal Road will cause one to arrive at only one destination. They will have entered Cultural Captivity.

6. Oil and Ice on the Slick Slope

The fact that cultural captivity exists is increasingly obvious. A retired Baptist minister who posts regularly on Facebook had the following entry on June 10, 2014: "A young family at the Southern Baptist Convention in Baltimore, Maryland indicated they just visited Washington DC and took the tour of the White House. To their utter shock, there were posters and signs at various places celebrating the gay lifestyle. They were shocked and offended…" The ground swell continues for the legalization of same gender and transgender marriages. The LGBT is a very small minority of the population. In the world at this time, it seems as though many things are upside down. The things which ought to be our focus and have our attention don't. Those things which represent a cross-section of aberrant lifestyle choices do gain one's attention.

Further evidence of cultural captivity taking place is a headline in the Washington Times on June 9, 2014: "Transgendered priest to give sermon at Washington National Cathedral." The body of the article includes: "The most visible Episcopal Church in the United States is hosting its first openly transgender priest this month." The Dean of the Cathedral, the Rev. Gary Hall, said: "We at Washington National Cathedral are striving to send a message of love and affirmation, especially to LGBT (Lesbian, Gay, Bi-Sexual, Transgender) youth who suffer daily because of their gender identity or sexual orientation…We want to proclaim to them as proudly and unequivocally as we can: 'Your gender identity is good and your sexual orientation is good because that's the way that God made you.' The General Convention of the Episcopal Church in 2012 approved the ordination of transgender persons. The convention also approved a rite of blessing for same-sex unions, a decision that's been a major contributor to the fracturing of Episcopal congregations. The cathedral performs same-sex marriages." Does this represent the new witness, affirmation, endorsement and cultural compromise of a national entity, namely, the National Cathedral (Episcopal)? Are they endeavoring to be politically correct within the climate and advocacy of the nation's capitol? Would it not be better if they found it as an obligation to champion and state that which the Word of God proclaims?

These things along with many others remind one of the words in Jeremiah 23:9-14 (MSG), "My head is reeling, my limbs are limp, I'm staggering like a drunk, seeing double from too much wine. And all because of God, because of his holy words. Now for what God says regarding the lying prophets: Can you believe it? A country teeming with adulterers, faithless, promiscuous idolater-adulterers! They're a curse on the land. The land is a wasteland. Their unfaithfulness is turning the country into a cesspool, prophets and priests devoted to desecration. They have nothing to do with me as their God. My very own Temple, mind you is mud-spattered with their crimes. God's Decree: But they won't get by with it. They'll find themselves on a slippery slope careening into the darkness, somersaulting into the pitch-black dark. I'll make them pay for their crimes. It will be the Year of Doom. God's Decree: Over in Samaria I saw prophets acting like silly fools. Shocking! They preached using that no-god Baal for a text, messing with the minds of my people. And the Jerusalem prophets are even worse. Horrible, sex-driven, living a lie, subsidizing a culture of wickedness, and never giving it a second thought. They're as bad as those wretches in old Sodom, the degenerates of old Gomorrah."

The issue of Sodom and Gomorrah is referenced at different times in the New Testament. On one occasion, as Jesus is sending His disciples to minister in His name, He gives them this word of instruction in Matthew 10:14-15, "And whoever shall not receive you, nor hear your words, as you go forth out of that house or that city, shake off the dust of your feet. Verily I say unto you, It shall be more tolerable for the land of Sodom and Gomorrah in the day of judgment, than for that city." The thrust is that the citizens who inhabited the cities of Sodom and Gomorrah were resistant to anything that pertained to God, His standard, moral values and foundational principles. The application is obvious. Anyone refusing the message and messengers who represent Jesus Christ and His

Gospel are viewed equivalently with the cities that were judged severely by God in the day of Abraham.

Once again, when Jesus is pronouncing the woes upon the various localities that have rejected Him and His message, He states in Matthew 11:23-24 (NKJV), "And you, Capernaum, who are exalted to heaven, will be brought down to Hades; for if the mighty works which were done in you had been done in Sodom, it would have remained until this day. But I say to you that it shall be more tolerable for the land of Sodom in the day of judgment than for you." The sin and rebellion factors are never menial in God's sight nor are they ever treated in a frivolous way or as something that is trivial or excusable. If our nation, world, culture and society think differently, there will be incalculable and unmeasurable consequences awaiting those who have ignored God and despised His Word. The most descriptive of the pronouncement of the impending judgment is stated in Jude 1:3-7 (NKJV), "Beloved, while I was very diligent to write to you concerning our common salvation, I found it necessary to write to you exhorting you to contend earnestly for the faith which was once for all delivered to the saints. For certain men have crept in unnoticed, who long ago were marked out for this condemnation, ungodly men, who turn the grace of our God into lewdness and deny the only Lord God and our Lord Jesus Christ. But I want to remind you, though you once knew this, that the Lord, having saved the people out of the land of Egypt, afterward destroyed those who did not believe. And the angels who did not keep their proper domain, but left their own abode. He has reserved in everlasting chains under darkness for the judgment of the great day; as Sodom and Gomorrah, and the cities around them in a similar manner to these, having given themselves over to sexual immorality and gone after strange flesh, are set forth as an example, suffering the vengeance of eternal fire."

For those living their lives on the edge, the wake-up call of Jude is very descriptive and clear. How can the National Cathedral or the LGBT ignore or rationalize the precise words that occasion the severest judgment of God, "(They have)...given themselves over to sexual immorality and gone after strange flesh...?" The church at large that has become shy about these issues lest they be thought to be judging others, how will they explain their efforts to finesse these matters and avoid taking a Biblical stand about them? One can also wonder about what judgment God will mete out on those who have compromised and failed to take a stand for Him and His Word! It is not a pretty or pleasant contemplation. The church needs to be guarded lest it allows itself to be numbered with those who have lost ability to be ashamed because of their sin or to blush because of unseemly behavior.

We can gain some insight into the mind of God when He had His prophet Jeremiah issue a warning of impending judgment upon the inhabitants of Jerusalem. The prophet's words from The Lord in Jeremiah 6:7-15 (NKJV) include: "As a well keeps its water fresh, so she keeps fresh her evil; violence and destruction are heard within her…Be warned…Jerusalem, lest I turn from you in disgust, lest I make you a desolation, an uninhabited land…To whom shall I speak and give warning, that they may hear? Behold, their ears are uncircumcised, they cannot listen; behold, the word of the Lord is to them an object of scorn; they take no pleasure in it…For from the least to the greatest of them, everyone is greedy for unjust gain; and from prophet to priest, everyone deals falsely. They have healed the wound of my people lightly, saying, Peace, Peace, when there is no peace. Were they ashamed when they committed abomination? No, they were not at all ashamed; they did not know how to blush. Therefore they shall fall among those who fall; at the time that I punish them, they shall be overthrown, says the Lord."

Emphasis points being made touch on: (1) "their ears are uncircumcised, they cannot listen; behold, the word of the Lord is to them an object of scorn; they take no pleasure in it…" The Word of God and His Truth are not viewed as being vital or necessary by the people and their leaders, both spiritual and political. Why would a supposedly religious people arrive at a point where the word of the Lord is to them an object of scorn; they take no pleasure in it? Has our nation, culture and society assumed this posture allowing the Word of God to be treated as an object of scorn? Has our nation, culture and society assumed a posture of ridicule regarding the Word of God and identify with those who take no pleasure in it? Are we no longer able to be ashamed or to blush about that which God designates as an abomination to Him? Additionally, (2) "For from the least to the greatest of them, everyone is greedy for unjust gain; and from prophet to priest, everyone deals falsely." The condemnation is due to a sad reality: (a) everyone is greedy for unjust gain, and (b) everyone deals falsely. Once again, The Lord sees this as an area where few are ashamed and most are insensitive to a point where they have lost their ability to blush. Their conscience has been seared and their spiritual discernment has disappeared.

Similar words are repeated in Jeremiah 8:7-12 (NKJV), "My people do not know the judgment of the Lord. How can you say: We are wise, and the law of the Lord is with us? Look, the false pen of the scribe certainly works falsehood. The wise men are ashamed. They are dismayed and taken. Behold, they have rejected the word of the Lord; so what wisdom do they have? Therefore I will give their wives to others, and their fields to those who will inherit them; because from the least even to the greatest everyone is given to covetousness; from the prophet even to the priest everyone deals falsely... Were they ashamed when they had committed abomination? No! They were not at all ashamed, nor did they know how to blush. Therefore they shall fall among those who fall; in the time of their punishment they shall be cast down, says the Lord." The indictment from the Lord is scathing. He takes note that (a) from the least even to the greatest everyone is given to covetousness; and (b) from the prophet even to the priest everyone deals falsely. There is a total breakdown within the culture about fairness and equity, as well as a disregard for accuracy and truth. The focus on covetousness is important for at least two reasons: (1) it is a violation of the tenth commandment, and (2) it constitutes idolatry in God's sight.

God has comprehensively stated His parameters regarding coveting. Exodus 20:17 (NKJV), The Lord established: "You shall not covet your neighbor's house; you shall not covet your neighbor's wife, nor his male servant, nor his female servant, nor his ox, nor his donkey, nor anything that is your neighbor's." To covet means: "to desire wrongfully, inordinately, or without due regard for the rights of others." With disregard of God's Law, Jeremiah records that an entire generation and people had fallen into the snare of coveting. Another aspect of coveting and why it is so repugnant in God's sight is stated in Colossians 4:5-7 (ESV): "Put to death therefore what is earthly in you: sexual immorality, impurity, passion, evil desire, and covetousness, which is idolatry. On account of these the wrath of God is coming. In these you too once walked, when you were living in them." New life in Christ means that certain things must be put to death if one is to walk with integrity before the Lord. A key phrase is: "… covetousness, which is idolatry." Idolatry is abhorrent to a holy God and He wants His people to put it to death. There is no room within God's Word and Standard that allows for variation or compromise with this principle. Is there hope for the nation, world, culture and society that has placed itself on the slippery slope?

Once a nation, world, culture or society gains the status of being like Sodom and Gomorrah or worse, is there any hope of averting the judgment of God? Regardless of one's appeal to the love, mercy and grace of God, does that prevent God from executing His justice and judgment upon His creation? Are the hands of God tied in any way regarding eternal judgment and punishment? Where do you believe our nation, culture and society is in terms of the slippery slope? Are we (a) avoiding it, (b) ignoring the danger of it, (c) finding some appeal to it, (d) not sensing the peril and danger if one steps onto it? Do we as a culture realize the risk and danger of flaunting God's Word? Do we need a day of revival such as in the time of Ezra and Nehemiah when the Scrolls containing God's Law were found and read in the public square? It is foolhardy to approach the precipice of the slippery slope and to ignore the consequences for those who step onto it. It is incumbent for all of us to avoid placing ourselves near the snares of the evil one and among those whose lifestyle will result in Cultural Captivity.

7. A Learning Curve - Knowing God's Prerogatives

The prerogatives of God do not always find agreement with God's people. They usually think in terms of God's love, mercy and grace. God is not restricted to or confined by His love, mercy and grace. His will and purpose is also motivated and governed by His holiness, justice and righteousness. Question and Answer 4 in the Westminster Shorter Catechism indicates: "God is a spirit, infinite, eternal, and unchangeable, in his being, wisdom, power, holiness, justice, goodness and truth." It is not all of what or who God is but it does suggest some areas of God's being and totality.

What is a prerogative? It is defined as: "an exclusive right, privilege limited to a specific person…" God, as The Creator of the universe, has reserved to Himself the sole authority and right to do that which He deems appropriate and best for His world and universe. He is not detached or absentminded when it comes to His creation. He has an eternal plan and purpose for all things. God is omniscient. He knows everything past, present and future. He is never caught off-guard or by surprise. Some might wonder: (1) Did the choice made by Adam and Eve in the Garden of Eden catch God by surprise? (2) Did the extent of the wickedness that escalated in the days of Noah find God preoccupied with other things? (3) Did the degree of perversion and degradation in Sodom and Gomorrah indicate that God was unaware of the behavior there? An overriding factor that attaches itself to these questions is stated in I Peter 1:18-22 (NKJV) "knowing that you were not redeemed with corruptible things, like silver or gold, from your aimless conduct received by tradition from your fathers, but with the precious blood of Christ, as of a lamb without blemish and without spot. He indeed was foreordained before the foundation of the world, but was manifest in these last times for you who through Him believe in God, who raised Him from the dead and gave Him glory, so that your faith and hope are in God." God's Word states that the plan of redemption was in place before the world or universe was created.

In Romans 9:15-24 (NKJV), Paul gives explanation to the prerogatives of God when he wrote: "For He (God) says to Moses: I will have mercy on whomever I will have mercy, and I will have compassion on whomever I will have compassion. So then it is not of him who wills, nor of him who runs, but of God who shows mercy. For the Scripture says to Pharaoh: For this very purpose I have raised you up, that I may show My power in you, and that My name may be declared in all the earth. Therefore He has mercy on whom He wills, and whom He wills He hardens. You will say to me then: Why does He still find fault? For who has resisted His will? But indeed, O man, who are you to reply against God? Will the thing formed say to him who formed it: Why have you made me like this? Does not the potter have power over the clay, from the same lump to make one vessel for honor and another for dishonor? What if God, wanting to show His wrath and to make His power known, endured with much long-suffering the vessels of wrath prepared for destruction, and that He might make known the riches of His glory on the vessels of mercy, which He had prepared beforehand for glory, even us..." God has an eternal plan in operation. It doesn't react or change according to events as they unfold. God's Plan is not adjusted based upon Opinion Polls and Surveys within the church or culture. The Alpha and Omega is The One who has planned and determined all things. He already knows the beginning and the ending of all that He has created.

An interesting exchange between Abraham and God about His plan for Sodom and Gomorrah is given in Genesis 18:17-33. "And the Lord said: Shall I hide from Abraham what I am doing, since Abraham shall surely become a great and mighty nation, and all the nations of the earth shall be blessed in him?...And the Lord said: Because the outcry against Sodom and Gomorrah is great, and because their sin is very grave...Abraham still stood before the Lord." Does God care about the world, nation, culture and society at any given point in human history? Does He arrive at a conclusion of what will and will not be allowed? The Plan of God is to destroy

Sodom and Gomorrah and the surrounding towns. Homosexuality is rampant and disregard of God's word prevails. Abraham is concerned because of his nephew (Lot) and his family. They live in that place and have adapted as best they could. It is at this point that we read: "And Abraham came near and begins a dialogue with God, Would You also destroy the righteous with the wicked? Suppose there were fifty righteous within the city; would You also destroy the place and not spare it for the fifty righteous that were in it? Far be it from You to do such a thing as this, to slay the righteous with the wicked, so that the righteous should be as the wicked; far be it from You! Shall not the Judge of all the earth do right?"

    Does Abraham believe he can change the mind of God? Is Abraham's appeal based upon what is humanly fair or that which is heavenly just? Is Abraham mildly challenging God when he states: "Far be it from You to do such a thing as this, to slay the righteous with the wicked?" Does Abraham have a precise understanding of God's being, nature and character? Will God view Abraham's approach as one that is trying His patience, or an opportunity for him to learn the prerogatives of God and why He does what He does? The text continues with the Lord responding kindly and patiently: "So the Lord said: If I find in Sodom fifty righteous within the city, then I will spare all the place for their sakes." Abraham will continue to lower the number in order for the cities to be spared. He inquires about if there are only 45 righteous, 40 and all the way down to 10. The Lord said reassuringly to Abraham: "I will not destroy it for the sake of ten." This will end the dialogue. We read: "So the Lord went His way as soon as He had finished speaking with Abraham; and Abraham returned to his place." God's plan will be implemented in God's time and on the basis of His holiness, justice and righteousness. When this plan is executed, it will become an illustration and instruction for all other people in all generations. God's Standard does not change according to human trends and aspirations. It is not impacted or influenced by political fiat. It is not altered by secular courts or popular votes. God's judgment is never enacted on the basis of the emotions and consensus of mankind. It is always based upon His will and purpose, His standard and character.

There is another interesting aspect to this account regarding Sodom and Gomorrah in Genesis 19:17-25. Despite the fact of what God had declared His plan and purpose for the cities, Lot was reluctant to leave that place. It had become home for him and his family. The text is interesting. The Word from the Lord comes to Lot: "Escape for your life! Do not look behind you nor stay anywhere in the plain. Escape to the mountains, lest you be destroyed. Then Lot said: Please, no...Indeed now, your servant has found favor in your sight, and you have increased your mercy which you have shown me by saving my life; but I cannot escape to the mountains, lest some evil overtake me and I die." Lot is attempting to institute a substitute plan for God's plan. Why do we tend to think that our Plan B sounds better than God's Plan A for us?

Lot's alternative plan was: See now, this city is near enough to flee to, and it is a little one; please let me escape there and my soul shall live. One issue is that Lot has no sense of urgency. The word of the Lord is to "Hurry Up." However, Lot wants to dialogue and make suggestions or amendments to God's plan. The word from the Lord is: "See, I have favored you concerning this thing also, in that I will not overthrow this city for which you have spoken. Hurry, escape there. For I cannot do anything until you arrive there." God's Plan will not be thwarted. Lot needs to gather up his family and possessions and move on out. Enough talk and delay. The text continues: "the name of the city was called Zoar. The sun had risen upon the earth when Lot entered Zoar."

Finally, the Lord will execute His plan and judgment. The text states: "Then the Lord rained brimstone and fire on Sodom and Gomorrah, from the Lord out of the heavens. So He overthrew those cities, all the plain, all the inhabitants of the cities, and what grew on the ground." There is a sad result and consequence. Lot and his family was supposed to look straight ahead and be focused on where they were going. This was not a time to look back at where they had been. However, Genesis 19:26 indicates: "But his wife looked back behind him, and she became a pillar of salt."

Trending Toward Cultural Captivity

In his notes on Luke 17:32, "Remember Lot's wife." J. C. Ryle stated: "There are few warnings in Scripture more solemn than this. The Lord Jesus Christ says to us, Remember Lot's wife. Lot's wife was a professor of religion: her husband was a righteous man (II Peter 2:8). She left Sodom with him on the day when Sodom was destroyed; she looked back towards the city from behind her husband, against God's express command; she was struck dead at once, and turned into a pillar of salt. And the Lord Jesus Christ holds her up as a beacon to His church: He says, Remember Lot's wife. It is a solemn warning, when we think of the person Jesus names. He does not bid us remember Abraham, or Isaac, or Jacob, or Sarah, or Hannah, or Ruth. No! He singles out one whose soul was lost for ever. He cries to us, Remember Lot's wife. It is a solemn warning, when we consider the subject Jesus is upon. He is speaking of His own second coming to judge the world: He is describing the awful state of unreadiness in which many will be found. The last days are on His mind, when He says, Remember Lot's wife. It is a solemn warning, when we think of the Person who gives it. The Lord Jesus is full of love, mercy, and compassion. He is One who will not break the bruised reed nor quench the smoking flax. He could weep over unbelieving Jerusalem, and pray for the men that crucified Him; yet even He thinks it good to give this solemn warning and remind us of lost souls. Even He says, Remember Lot's wife. It is a solemn warning, when we think of the persons to whom it was first given. The Lord Jesus was speaking to His disciples. He was not addressing the Scribes and Pharisees who hated him, but Peter, James, and John, and many others who loved Him: yet even to them He thinks good to address a caution. Even to them He says, Remember Lot's wife. It is a solemn warning, when we consider the manner in which it was given. He does not merely say, Beware of following-take heed of imitating-do not be like Lot's wife. He uses a different word. He says, Remember. He speaks as if we were all in danger of forgetting the subject; He stirs up our lazy memories; He bids us keep the case before our minds. He cries, Remember Lot's wife."

Is God ignoring the events of our times? No! Is He indifferent toward the trends and practices within the world, nation, culture and society? No! Is He unaware of those who eagerly approach and promote the slippery slope? No! Will God ignore the endorsed and legalized practices of this nation (or any nation)? No! Is Psalm 9:17, "The wicked shall be turned into hell, and all the nations that forget God" viable and functional for these times? Yes! If innocent people are trapped in Cultural Captivity, will God know where they are and care for them accordingly? Yes! Can we determine how and when God will respond to those who scorn Him and His Word? No! Are we confident that He will deal with them as and how He pleases, when and where He pleases? Yes!

In the learning curve, one will gain knowledge and insight into the prerogatives, mind, will and purpose of Almighty God. Micah 5:8 instructs us how we should live until the great day of our Lord: "He has shown you...what is good; and what does the Lord require of you but to do justly, to love mercy, and to walk humbly with your God!" Living apart from this requirement places one within the Trend Toward Cultural Captivity.

8. A Bent Bugle

If the one who has been assigned to appear at a formal ceremony to play Taps arrived in full military dress carrying a bent bugle, it would be viewed as an oddity and unacceptable. It would be an insult to the guests who had assembled with the expectation that dignity and respect would be the order of the day. Additionally, if an effort was made to play the bent bugle during the ceremony, the ensuing sound would be adding insult to that solemn gathering. A fact of protocol is that it would be better to appear without the bugle than to treat the occasion or to approach it in a carefree, indifferent and matter-of-fact manner. The military not only expects more from their personnel - they require and demand more as well.

When the Church bearing the name of Jesus Christ is involved in its assigned task, the expectations and demands are no less than at a military ceremony. When a controversy arose in the Corinthian Church regarding the seeking and demonstrating of spiritual gifts, Paul responded in I Corinthians 14:7-8 with a reference to musical instruments and the expectation one has when hearing an instrument played. Paul wrote (ESV): "If even lifeless instruments, such as the flute or the harp, do not give distinct notes, how will anyone know what is played? And if the bugle gives an indistinct sound, who will get ready for battle?" In the MSG paraphrase, "If musical instruments, such as flutes or harps, aren't played so that each note is distinct and in tune, how will anyone be able to catch the melody and enjoy the music? If the trumpet (bugle) call can't be distinguished, will anyone show up for the battle?"

On Facebook, there was a discussion pertaining to corporation and product name-changes, and how that might apply to a name-change for the church in the twenty-first century. The corporation may change its name due to some negative perceptions about its products or operation. There would be little changes with the day-to-day operation or product content. It would be done to divert attention away from the negatives. The consideration with name-change for the Church is a different matter. It can be an attempt to alter some negatives in the minds of the general public. Another reason is to become more attractive and appealing to the general public. The rationale for some churches is to use a church name that is more neutral or generic than one containing a denominational affiliation or a doctrinal persuasion. Amid this discussion, one possible name-change that surfaced was that the modern church could be called "The Chameleon Church." The reasoning attached to the name change was because "it changes to fit its surroundings and never stands out from its environment." Is that fair and applicable to the twenty-first century church? Is such a designation deserved? How does today's church explain itself in a clearly defined way? When I was a boy, we attended a church that had engraved the focus and purpose of ministry in stone above the entry way. It read: "We preach Christ - crucified, risen and coming again." It was definitive and unequivocal. Those who proclaimed the Word of the Lord from the pulpit were expected and required to consistently represent that message and purpose to all. A church needs to have a clearly defined message and purpose based upon The Word of God. Anything less than that will be like the bent bugle that gives an uncertain sound.

    This is a major emphasis when observations about the churches is given in Revelation 2 and 3. Jesus sets out to define the church as he sees it and the remedy that is necessary to be functional and truly represent of Him. Revelation 2:1-7 (ASV), "To the angel of the church in Ephesus write: These things saith he that holds the seven stars in his right hand, he that walks in the midst of the seven golden candlesticks: I know thy works, and thy toil and patience, and that thou canst not bear evil men, and didst try them that call themselves apostles, and they are not, and didst find them false; and thou hast patience and didst bear for my name's sake, and hast not grown weary. But I have [this] against thee, that thou didst leave thy first love. Remember therefore whence thou art fallen, and repent and do the first works; or else I come to thee, and will move thy candlestick out of its place, except thou repent. But this thou hast, that you hate the works of the Nicolaitans, which I also hate.

He that hath an ear, let him hear what the Spirit saith to the churches. To him that overcomes, to him will I give to eat of the tree of life, which is in the Paradise of God."

Jesus comments on all of the positives that the Ephesian Church has done and is doing. He commends them for their effort and participation. He also makes particular reference to the Nicolaitans. While not much mention is made of the Nicolaitans in Scripture, they are mentioned twice in Revelation 2. The general concern with this negative influence in the church was their tolerance toward and practice of (1) fornication and (2) eating food that had been sacrificed to idols. *The International Standard Bible Encyclopedia* (ISBE) states: "The problem underlying the Nicolaitan controversy, though so little direct mention is made of it in Scripture, was in reality most important, and concerned the whole relation of Christianity to paganism and its usages. The Nicolaitans disobeyed the command issued to the Gentile churches, by the apostolic council held at Jerusalem in 49-50 AD, that they should refrain from the eating of "things sacrificed to idols" (Acts 15:29). Such a restriction, though seemingly hard, in that it prevented the Christian communities from joining in public festivals, and so brought upon them suspicion and dislike, was yet necessary to prevent a return to a pagan laxity of morals. To this danger the Nicolaitans were themselves a glaring witness, and therefore John was justified in condemning them."

The Nicolaitans were the bent bugle of their day in the Church. Jesus commends the Ephesians for having ignored their teaching and refusing to have any part with them and their espoused inclinations and teaching. However, the church at Pergamum is a different story. In Revelation 2:14-16, Jesus observed: "But I have a few things against thee, because thou hast there some that hold the teaching of Balaam, who taught Balak to cast a stumbling-block before the children of Israel, to eat things sacrificed to idols, and to commit fornication. So hast thou also some that hold the teaching of the Nicolaitans in like manner. Repent therefore; or else I come to thee quickly, and I will make war against them with the sword of my mouth." Not only had the bent bugle of Balaam and the Nicolaitans gained attention and a following, but the church name could have easily been changed to The Chameleon Church. It allowed itself to be whatever the people wanted it to be and adapted itself to the customs and practices of the day. Rather than remaining a beacon of light, it had allowed itself to become a citadel of darkness.

An application of this designation is contained in Francis Berger's Blog posted in February 2014, in which he observes and comments: "In my novel *The City of Earthly Desire*, the hedonist Anthony Vergil, who spent his formative years attending the finest schools the United Kingdom has to offer, frequently and rather scornfully refers to universities as Citadels of Darkness. I must admit that Verge's view of post-secondary institutions of higher learning are, for the most part, a reflection of my own. There was a time I considered universities to be Ivory Towers, but my experiences in education, both as a student and as a teacher, have led me to the conclusion that the Ivory Tower ideal most people hold to be true is a sham. Far from being Ivory Towers, most universities today have become, as Anthony Vergil vehemently insists, veritable "Citadels of Darkness." If this Blog is making a valid point regarding institutions of higher learning, what parallel point can be made about the church? If the Ivory Towers of education have employed the use of a bent bugle that summon people to participate in a Citadel of Darkness, how greater is this truth when it is applied to the Church? Rather than standing as The Temple of the Living God, it has allowed itself to become tolerant of that which is repugnant to God, and is now more committed to being The Chameleon Church, a Citadel of Darkness.

Jesus addressed this issue in Matthew 6:22-24, "The lamp of the body is the eye: if therefore thine eye be single, thy whole body shall be full of light. But if thine eye be evil, thy whole body shall be full of darkness. If therefore the light that is in thee be darkness, how great is the darkness! No man can serve two masters; for either he will hate the one, and love the other; or else he will hold to one, and despise the other." The words in verse 23 are vivid and descriptive, "if the light that is in you is darkness, how great is the darkness!" Jesus is making a declaration about the darkness. It is not a rhetorical question but a statement of fact. The sad plight of The Chameleon Church is stated by Jesus in John 5:39-40, "You search the Scriptures, because you think that in them ye have eternal life; and these are they which bear witness of me; and you will not come to me, that ye may have life." The Chameleon Church allows people to think they have eternal life. Jesus states this is untrue. If one refuses to come to Jesus Christ and embrace Him as Savior and Lord, he does not have eternal life. This is the emphatic statement given in I John 5:10-13, "He that believes on the Son of God hath the witness in him: he that believes not God hath made him a liar; because he hath not believed in the witness that God hath borne concerning his Son. And the witness is this, that God gave unto us eternal life, and this life is in his Son. He that has the Son has the life; he that has not the Son of God has not the life. These things have I written unto you, that ye may know that ye have eternal life, unto you that believe on the name of the Son of God." It cannot be stated more in a more clear cut and plain manner.

When Paul is giving his defense and testimony in Acts 26:16-20, he references the words he heard from Jesus Christ on the road to Damascus: "But arise, and stand upon thy feet: for to this end have I appeared unto thee, to appoint thee a minister and a witness both of the things wherein thou hast seen me, and of the things wherein I will appear unto thee; delivering thee from the people, and from the Gentiles, unto whom I send thee, to open their eyes, that they may turn from darkness to light and from the power of Satan unto God, that they may receive remission of sins and an inheritance among them that are sanctified by faith in me. Wherefore, O king Agrippa, I was not disobedient unto the heavenly vision: but declared both to them of Damascus first and at Jerusalem, and throughout all the country of Judaea, and also to the Gentiles, that they should repent and turn to God, doing works worthy of repentance." His assigned mission was stated in the words "to open their eyes, that they may turn from darkness to light and from the power of Satan unto God."

Many years ago, a servant of the Lord was explaining a similar issue for those who have listened to the bent bugle and followed the uncertain sound. The subject was about having faith in faith. His approach, while pithy, made the point that faith in faith was like a blind man walking in the dark and crossing over a bridge that doesn't reach the other side. The Chameleon Church has expertise when it comes to making sounds with a bent bugle. People can be persuaded that the uncertain sound of the bent bugle is how the bugle is supposed to sound. They are given a sense of feeling good about themselves, being joyful, and having hope for the future. However, they have become like the blind man crossing the bridge in the dark that doesn't reach the other side. John 8:12 (NLT) records the words of Jesus to the people, "I am the light of the world. If you follow me, you won't be stumbling through the darkness, because you will have the light that leads to life." The choice is clear. One can follow the sounds coming from a bent bugle, and stumble through the darkness, or heed the sound emanating from an unbent bugle and have the light that leads to life. Which Bugle are you following - the one that leads to Cultural Captivity or the one that leads to eternal life?

9. Mind Renewal

The Scriptures make reference to the mind of a person especially in terms of commitment and renewal. Philippians 2:5 indicates: "Have this mind in you, which was also in Christ Jesus." What does that mean in practical terms? When the Good Samaritan inquired how he might inherit eternal life, Jesus said to him in Luke 10:27, "You shall love the Lord your God with all your heart and with all your soul and with all your strength and with all your mind, and your neighbor as yourself." How does one begin to love the Lord with all of one's heart, soul, strength and mind? In His design and purpose for His disciples, Jesus sets forth a standard of discipleship in Luke 14:26-33 (NLT). He uses the term "cannot" three times in his requirement for disciples. First, verse 26, "Anyone who comes to me but refuses to let go of father, mother, spouse, children, brothers, sisters…yes, even one's own self! He cannot be my disciple." There is no place or room for divided loyalty or distraction. Second, verse 27, "Anyone who won't shoulder his own cross and follow behind me cannot be my disciple." The idea expressed by Jesus is that complete abandonment to Him is basic and necessary. The Cross is the symbol of your life's purpose, mission and message. Third, verse 33, "Simply put, if you're not willing to take what is dearest to you, whether plans or people, and kiss it good-bye, you cannot be my disciple." It means that there can be no looking back at what was or might've been. There is to be no room for regret or wistful, wishful thinking.

Jesus was aware of the human mind and its inclinations. He addressed this in his description given in Luke 17:28-33, "Likewise even as it came to pass in the days of Lot; they ate, they drank, they bought, they sold, they planted, they built; but in the day that Lot went out from Sodom it rained fire and brimstone from heaven, and destroyed them all: after the same manner shall it be in the day that the Son of man is revealed. In that day, he that shall be on the housetop, and his goods in the house, let him not go down to take them away: and let him that is in the field likewise not return back. Remember Lot's wife. Whosoever shall seek to gain his life shall lose it: but whosoever shall lose his life shall preserve it." What did Jesus mean and imply when He said, Remember Lot's wife? What does Lot's wife have to do with people living in the twenty-first century? Was there something lacking in her mind-renewal or readiness to head in a new direction for her life? Did she possess a mindset that was more interested in where she had been rather than where she was going?

What did Jesus want people in all generations to remember when He said in Matthew 24:12, "And because iniquity shall be multiplied, the love of the many shall wax cold. but he that endures to the end, the same shall be saved?" Mind renewal includes the ability one has in terms of perception. The Matthew passage seems to indicate that the loss of spiritual strength and power can occur in such a way that it is imperceptible. In the previous chapter, the discussion focused on The Chameleon Church and the bent bugle sending forth uncertain sounds. The subtle loss of spiritual awareness, sensitivity and commitment occurs as pressures of conformity and compromise crowd in and one's faith is challenged to a point where it gradually erodes and disappears. The cautionary words of Hebrews 4:1-2 are applicable here: "Let us fear therefore, lest haply, a promise being left of entering into his rest, any one of you should seem to have come short of it. For indeed we have had good tidings preached unto us, even as also they: but the word of hearing did not profit them, because it was not united by faith with them that heard." Just think of the possibility and potential of people hearing the Gospel and the Word of God repeatedly but to no profit. Why? They heard the word of God but they failed to unite it with faith. They did not appropriate it and believe it. They were comfortable with what they heard but failed to respond to it and make the vital commitment to Christ and His Kingdom.

A basic challenge to Mind-Renewal is given in Romans 12:1-3. Paul wrote: "I beseech you therefore, brethren, by the mercies of God, to present your bodies a living sacrifice, holy, acceptable to God, which is your spiritual service. And be not fashioned according to this world: but be transformed by the renewing of your mind, and may prove what is the good and acceptable and perfect will of God. For I say, through the grace that was given me, to every man that is among you, not to think of himself more highly than he ought to think; but to think as to think soberly, according as God hath dealt to each man a measure of faith." A point of emphasis is the phrase that states: "…be transformed by the renewing of your mind." Paul held out the hope that a change in one's thinking, predispositions, attitudes, mindsets and commitments is possible. Just because one has started in life negatively does not mean that is the final disposition for the individual. Change, transformation and renewal of mind can occur in the living sacrifice process. How can this happen when some people are so set in their ways? Some people can be thought of as being rock-solid followers of Jesus Christ and suddenly behave in a manner contrary to what that lifestyle requires. How and why does this occur as a norm? An answer is that the living sacrifice requirements have been ignored. The possibilities for transformation are available but it will require personal commitment in order for it to be realized.

Sadly, within the church context, there is the presence of Spiritual Schizophrenia. From the secular point of view, there are all kinds of studies regarding schizophrenia. Schizophrenia was first described by German psychiatrist Emil Kraepelin in the 1890s. With the various studies and research, it continues to be a tragic and mysterious form of mental illness. The inner conflict and affliction is frightening for an individual. The person enduring this form of mental illness hears voices telling him/her varying data leaving one with the inability to tell what is real from what is imaginary. To the person with schizophrenia the voices and visions sound and look as authentic as a newscaster on television or some object in room. Slightly more than one percent of the population of the United States gropes with this condition. No one can accurately predict or calculate who will be afflicted with schizophrenia. Although the malady is thought to arise from neuron malfunction during fetal development, it becomes pronounced as a person arrives on the threshold of adulthood. A sad reality is that while treatment is improving, there is no cure on the horizon. It is difficult to even imagine the anguish of an individual and the inner turmoil as one endures and tries to cope with this malady.

Does the study of Schizophrenia find a place for a Spiritual component to it? The above secular conclusions indicate there is no cure in sight and no hope for the despairing soul who is trapped in his/her condition. What about those who struggle with spiritual schizophrenia? Is there any cure or hope for that person. What is it that Paul was instructing in Romans 12? Is he promoting an ideal or a reality? Paul often referred back to his former lifestyle prior to his encounter with Jesus Christ on the road to Damascus. Up to the point of encounter, he had demonstrated an obsessive type of behavior. He was known as Saul of Tarsus and his passion and compulsion was to reduce or eliminate those who were followers of Jesus Christ. The picture stated about his obsession and commitment is given in Acts 9:1-2, "But Saul, yet breathing threatening and slaughter against the disciples of the Lord, went unto the high priest, and asked of him letters to Damascus unto the synagogues, that if he found any that were of the Way, whether men or women, he might bring them bound to Jerusalem." The NLT paraphrase of these verses is, "Meanwhile, Saul was uttering threats with every breath. He was eager to destroy the Lord's followers, so he went to the high priest. He requested letters addressed to the synagogues in Damascus, asking their cooperation in the arrest of any followers of the Way he found there. He wanted to bring them -- both men and women -- back to Jerusalem in chains."

It would be fascinating to have a psychological profile of Saul prior to and following his conversion. One can only wonder if he was controlled by demonic forces as he carried out his obsessions. Jesus did open the door to that possibility when He addressed the Scribes and Pharisees and said in John 8:43-46, "Why do you not understand my speech? Even because ye cannot hear my word. You are of your father the devil, and the lusts of your father it is your will to do. He was a murderer from the beginning, and stands not in the truth, because there is no truth in him. When he speaks a lie, he speaks of his own: for he is a liar, and the father thereof. But because I say the truth, you believe me not. Which of you convicts Me of sin? If I say truth, why do you not believe Me?" It is obvious here that Jesus was indicating that His opponents were identified with the devil and not with Almighty God. The position and title they held as religious leaders and teachers is meaningless. They had not believed or implemented the Word of God or belief in Him. Therefore, the conclusion drawn by Jesus identified them for what they were, namely, identified with and representing the devil and the devil's interests.

The fact of what we know for certain is that Saul of Tarsus was confronted by a great light and heard the voice of Jesus. He went down to the ground and was blinded. His life as a representative of everything that was hostile and evil toward Christ and His followers is abruptly halted. As he is assisted up and led into the city, he will soon realize a dramatic transformation occurring in his life and purpose. He was struck down as an enemy of Christ but rises up to become an emissary for Christ. He was struck down as one who was seeking to decrease the number of those in The Way but he rises up to be one who will labor to increase the number of converts and followers of Jesus Christ. He was struck down with letters authorizing the persecution and arrest of believers but he arises to become one who writes and sends letters of instruction and encouragement to the churches and younger ministers.

He knows that there is tremendous possibility and potential to the ones who will seek Christ and His way for their lives when he writes in Romans 12:1-3 regarding, (1) the benefit to one becoming a living sacrifice (an offering to God). The allusion is to the requirement for an atoning sacrifice. Only the best in its entirety should be placed on the altar as a sacrifice. (2) The purpose and possibility of being transformed by the renewing of one's mind. One does not need to be relegated to or remain in the status quo of life. God's grace will take the ordinary and make it into the extraordinary for God's eternal purpose. (3) The potential of being able to discern the good, acceptable and perfect will of God. To know the mind and will of God is indispensable for the one in relationship to Jesus Christ. Even as the Savior prayed, "Not my will but thine be done" in like manner, we must approach the Throne of our God.

Colossians 4:12 gives us a glimpse of a servant's heart as he prayed for the people of the church: "Epaphras, who is one of you, a servant of Christ Jesus, salutes you, always striving for you in his prayers, that ye may stand perfect and fully assured in all the will of God." We should have an equal concern that we will stand perfect, complete and fully assured in all the will of God. (4) The proper place for humility and sober thinking. The MSG paraphrase of Romans 12:1-3 expands on these verses somewhat: "So here's what I want you to do, God helping you: Take your everyday, ordinary life - sleeping, eating, going-to-work, and walking-around life - and place it before God as an offering. Embracing what God does for you is the best thing you can do for him. Don't become so well-adjusted to your culture that you fit into it without even thinking. Instead, fix your attention on God. You'll be changed from the inside out. Readily recognize what he wants from you, and quickly respond to it. Unlike the culture around you, always dragging you down to its level of immaturity, God brings the best out of you, develops well-formed maturity in you. I'm speaking to you out of deep gratitude for all that God has given me, and especially as I have responsibilities in relation to you. Living then, as every one of you does, in pure grace, it's important that you not misinterpret yourselves as people who are bringing this goodness to God. No, God brings it all to you. The only accurate way to understand ourselves is by what God is and by what he does for us, not by what we are and what we do for him."

This paraphrase expresses the parameters for Christian faith and practice. It is a clear and precise expression of that which is on the heart of God and what He wants to be on and in each of our hearts. Even as Jesus called disciples in His day with the words, "Follow Me, I will make you." He holds out the same possibility and potential for each of us today. Whatever God calls you to do for Him, you can be certain that He will equip and enable you for the task. Paul had this sense when he wrote in II Corinthians 2:14-

17 (ESV), "But thanks be to God, who in Christ always leads us in triumphal procession, and through us spreads the fragrance of the knowledge of him everywhere. For we are the aroma of Christ to God among those who are being saved and among those who are perishing, to one a fragrance from death to death, to the other a fragrance from life to life. Who is sufficient for these things? For we are not, like so many, peddlers of God's word, but as men of sincerity, as commissioned by God, in the sight of God we speak in Christ." With all of what he sees as his task for the Lord, he has a sense of his personal inadequacy when he asks: "Who is sufficient for these things?" However, he also has in mind the words: "But thanks be to God, who in Christ always leads us in triumphal procession." When one's sufficiency is in Jesus Christ, He will lead His people in triumphal procession. Being His people in triumphal procession, one will escape the hazards, pitfalls, risks and dangers of the Trend Toward Cultural Captivity. We will be a people who have counted the cost and are now joined with those whose song is: "I have decided to follow Jesus…No turning back; The Cross before me, the world behind me…No turning back; Though none go with me, still I will follow…No turning back."

10. What We Must Be

A Hymn written in 1806, "Praise The Savior, Ye Who Know Him," contains lyrics that are perceptive and interesting: "…He for conflict fits and arms us; Nothing moves and nothing harms us, While we trust in Him." In looking forward to when one's journey is ended, the Lyric is: "Then we shall be where we would be, Then we shall be what we should be, Things that are not now, nor could be, Soon shall be our own." Between the here and now as we journey forward to the there and then are a considerable number of lessons to be learned as we prepare for what we must be in this day and culture.

We've noted in II Corinthians 5:17 that one must be certain of where one is positionally. The text is clear: "If anyone is in Christ, he/she is a new creature." The MSG summarizes: "Now we look inside, and what we see is that anyone united with the Messiah gets a fresh start, is created new. The old life is gone; a new life burgeons!" J. B. Phillips renders the text: "For if a man/woman is in Christ he/she becomes a new person altogether - the past is finished and gone, everything has become fresh and new." Positionally that's where we are and who we are becoming by God's grace. When one becomes a new creation in Jesus Christ, it begins a process of growth and development that will require one's lifetime of commitment to begin to learn, grow and to become both like and usable for the Master.

The totality of what one must be if he is to be usable by The Master could fill volumes. It reminds one of a summary verse in John 20:30-31, "Many other signs therefore did Jesus in the presence of the disciples, which are not written in this book: but these are written, that you may believe that Jesus is the Christ, the Son of God; and that believing you may have life in his name." In other words, John is indicating that the things recorded in His Gospel and other Scriptures were not intended to be an exhaustive encyclopedia or a biography of everything Jesus said and did. He indicates that the content of Scriptural writing and The Gospels is sufficient for one to have a solid foundation and reason for believing in the Lord Jesus Christ and becoming a recipient of eternal life in Him.

    We glean from the Holy Scriptures what we must be is by His grace. There are at least seven key areas to consider. First and foremost, one must be His fully committed disciple. In Luke 14:25-33, Jesus lays down parameters regarding the cost of discipleship. He wants anyone considering discipleship to know the costs that will be exacted of one who desires to become a disciple of The Lord Jesus Christ. The cost Jesus indicates is threefold: (a) Christ is first in all things whereas family and self are secondary. If that is not the case, Jesus stated that one "cannot be My disciple." (b) Christ wants His followers to be identified with the crucified life. His words are clear and succinct (verse 27, ESV): "Whoever does not bear his own cross and come after me cannot be my disciple." In Luke 9:23 an important word is included: "And he said to all: "If anyone would come after me, let him deny himself and take up his cross daily and follow me." It is the word "daily" and the need for a 24/7 daily walk with Jesus Christ and total commitment to Him. The Apostle Paul understood the importance and meaningfulness of these words when he wrote in Galatians 2:20 (NKJV), "I have been crucified with Christ; it is no longer I who live, but Christ lives in me; and the life which I now live in the flesh I live by faith in the Son of God, who loved me and gave Himself for me." This commitment is expressed in a different way in Philippians 3:8-11, "I also count all things loss for the excellence of the knowledge of Christ Jesus my Lord, for whom I have suffered the loss of all things, and count them as rubbish, that I may gain Christ and be found in Him, not having my own righteousness, which is from the law, but that which is through faith in Christ, the righteousness which is from God by faith; that I may know Him and the power of His resurrection, and the fellowship of His sufferings, being conformed to His death, if, by any means, I may attain to the resurrection from the dead." (c) These words of Paul are an application of Luke 14:33 (ESV) where Jesus said: "So therefore, any one of you who does not renounce all that he has cannot be my disciple." The requirement for discipleship includes the difficult area that pertains to all of what one is and all of what one has/possesses. This is the clear and only pathway available for one to avoid and be delivered from a Cultural Captivity.

Second, God's call for one to follow Him (to be a disciple) is to the end that one will become a fisher for the souls of mankind. In His earthly ministry, the call of Jesus was issued to particular men for a particular task. In Matthew 4:18-22, as Jesus is walking, He sees four men to whom He said: "Follow Me, and I will make you to be fishers of men." The response of Peter, Andrew, James and John was immediate. They left their boats and nets and immediately began to follow Jesus. It would be a learning process to prepare them for kingdom objectives and work. Their individual personalities were varied. Peter was impetuous and bold; Andrew was reserved and perceptive, always bringing people to Jesus; James was marked by clarity and sound reasoning and judgment; John was marked by his tenderness and compassion. Jesus would go on to call others, such as Luke the Physician and Matthew the Tax Collector. Fishermen and professional men would be brought together for God's purposes to be carried out through them.

Third, a disciple must be attached to The Vine, Jesus Christ. In John 15:1-15, Jesus indicates that secular ranking or assumed spiritual prestige are not the determining factor in one who is called to be a disciple. There are at least four basic requirements: (a) Abiding in Christ the Vine/Christ, the Vine abiding in me. This indicates that spiritual growth and fruition result from that willing relationship with Him. It allows for the necessary pruning of anything that would corrupt the vine or diminish its fruitfulness. (b) Abiding in His Words and His Words abiding in the disciple. When this is ones status, it indicates an openness to both know and do the will of God in and through ones life. It also encourages the benefit of ones communion with Christ in Prayer. The affirmation is that: "you will ask what you desire, and it shall be done for you." (c)) Abiding in the love of Christ and His love flowing in and through the disciple. There is an important phrase appearing in Romans 12:9

that has different expression in various translations. Some of them are ESV: "Let love be genuine."; ASV: "Let love be without hypocrisy."; NLT: "Don't just pretend that you love others. Really love them."; KJV: "Let love be without dissimulation (feigning, hypocrisy)." MSG: "Love from the center of who you are; don't fake it." The parameters for His love flowing in and through us are indispensable for effective ministry being done for Jesus Christ. (d)) Abiding in His love infers and attaches it to Abiding in His Commandments. Why is this the case? What is Jesus stating at this point? Is it adherence and conformity to the Mosaic and ceremonial laws? Jesus clearly defines that which He has in mind in verses 12-14, 17: "This is My commandment, that you love one another as I have loved you. Greater love has no one than this, than to lay down one's life for his friends. You are My friends if you do whatever I command you...These things I command you, that you love one another." Are these things tedious for the disciple? Yes! Will they require considerable discipline in order to pursue these things? Yes! There is a benefit that Jesus attaches to this discourse. In verse 11, He states: "These things I have spoken to you, that My joy may remain in you, and that your joy may be full." It is difficult to either imagine or fathom all of what it means to have the joy of Jesus Christ is us and enabling us to have greater joy throughout our lives. This joy is far different and much greater than the happiness with which some are content. Happiness conveys the idea that circumstances and events can determine when one will be happy. Some events and circumstances result in sadness and sorrow, whereas others can result in happiness and gladness. The joy of the Lord depends exclusively on a personal relationship with and commitment to Jesus Christ. True joy is always relational whereas happiness is almost always circumstantial.

Fourth, the disciple must be endued by and with His Power. After His resurrection, Jesus appears to His disciples and does something very unique. John 20:19-22 states: "When therefore it was evening, on that day, the first day of the week, and when the doors were shut where the disciples were, for fear of the Jews, Jesus came and stood in the midst, and said unto them, Peace be unto you. And when he had said this, He showed them His hands and His side. The disciples were glad, when they saw the Lord. Jesus said to them again, Peace be unto you: as the Father hath sent me, even so send I you. And when He had said this, He breathed on them, and said unto them, Receive the Holy Spirit."

The unique act is when He breathed on them. It is unique because this similar phrasing not only appears here but also in two other unique situations. The first time the phrase appears is in Genesis 2:7, "And God formed man of the dust of the ground, and breathed into his nostrils the breath of life; and man became a living soul." Man was just an assembled form of dust and dirt until the unique moment when God breathed into the nostrils of this lifeless form and it became a living soul. The breath of God was the singular cause of life in that which was being made in the image of God (Genesis 1:26-27). Another place where this phrase is employed is in II Timothy 3:16 (ESV), "All Scripture is breathed out by God and profitable for teaching, for reproof, for correction, and for training in righteousness, that the man of God may be competent, equipped for every good work." If there was no breath of God attached to the words in the Bible, it would just be a book of words, interesting sayings and stories. However, once God's breath is attached to the words spoken and written, they have life and reality for the disciple. All of it, being God-breathed, then becomes profitable for teaching, reproof, correction and instruction in righteousness. When the *Westminster Shorter Catechism* No. 3 asks: "What do the Scriptures principally teach?", there is purpose, meaning and enthusiasm in the response: "The Scriptures principally teach what man is to believe concerning God, and what duty God requires of man." This is a true and valid response because God's breathing out the words has given every one of them life.

Fifth, the disciples must be His witnesses throughout the world. At the moment when Jesus Christ is about to ascend into heaven, He leaves these final words with His disciples in Acts 1:8-9 (NKJV), "…You shall receive power when the Holy Spirit has come upon you; and you shall be witnesses to Me in Jerusalem, and in all Judea and Samaria, and to the end of the earth. Now when He had spoken these things, while they watched, He was taken up, and a cloud received Him out of their sight." They were empowered to be his disciples and witnesses in Jerusalem, Judea, Samaria and to the end of the earth. Why did Jesus designate these places in the order that He did? A possible reason would include the following: (1) Jerusalem was where they were and the place of their greatest failure. They needed to begin there before they went anywhere else. (2) Judea was a vast expanse of land. It was an outreach to their country that would require long and arduous travel through some remote and isolated places. (3) John Gill writes in his commentary: "Samaria was a place where Christ had before forbid His disciples to go; but now their commission is enlarged, and they are sent there; and here Philip went upon the persecution raised against the church at Jerusalem, and preached Christ with great success, to the conversion of many; Peter and John went to lay their hands on them, and confirm them; see (Acts 8:5,14). Another reason for going to Samaria may be to build a bridge to a people with whom there had been a mutual disdain and animosity. They would now be ministering to them in Christ's name and including them to hear the Gospel message."

Sixth, a disciple must be His ambassador. The clearest presentation of this is given in II Corinthians 5:18-20 (NKJV), "Now all things are of God, who has reconciled us to Himself through Jesus Christ, and has given us the ministry of reconciliation, that is, that God was in Christ reconciling the world to Himself, not imputing their trespasses to them, and has committed to us the word of reconciliation. Now then, we are ambassadors for Christ, as though God were pleading through us: we implore you on Christ's behalf, be reconciled to God." The task of the Ambassador is clearly defined: "We are ambassadors for Christ, as though God were pleading through us: we implore you on Christ's behalf, be reconciled to God." We are to make the message of the Gospel available to all as we plead with all types, races, nationalities - both hostile to non-hostile - be reconciled to the one true God. That message must not be diluted or modified in any manner. In Christ, we are God's representatives in a troubled world where many have entered into Cultural Captivity. The Ambassador's message must be given with precision, clarity and boldness - Be Reconciled To God. Paul's request for prayer in Ephesians 6:19-20 underscores his commitment to being the ambassador that will be effective when he wrote: "Pray for…me, that words may be given to me in opening my mouth boldly to proclaim the mystery of the gospel, for which I am an ambassador in chains, that I may declare it boldly, as I ought to speak." The desire of Paul was to be an ambassador of Jesus Christ at all times and in all circumstances.

Seventh, the disciple must be filled with the Holy Spirit. Ephesians 5:17-18 (NKJV) indicates to the disciple of the Lord Jesus Christ, "do not be unwise, but understand what the will of the Lord is. And do not be drunk with wine, in which is dissipation; but be filled with the Spirit." The idea is that one is not to be influenced or controlled by anything or anyone except the Holy Spirit of God. Being filled with the Holy Spirit requires a particular behavioral pattern on the part of the disciple. Ephesians 4:30-32 (NKJV) gives a partial reason and guideline: "And do not grieve the Holy Spirit of God, by whom you were sealed for the day of redemption. Let all bitterness, wrath, anger, clamor, and evil speaking be put away from you, with all malice. And be kind to one another, tenderhearted, forgiving one another, just as God in Christ forgave you." In this day and time, we need to consider whether or not we are part of the solution or part of the ongoing problem. Cultural Captivity is a real and present danger. As Ambassadors for Jesus Christ, we must enter those embattled places where one's best effort may be met with hostility and resistance. It might entail personal suffering and cost. The King of kings and Lord of lords who has commissioned us to be His Ambassadors expects us to be unabashed and unafraid as we go in His name. Can He count on you to fulfill your assigned task or will He see you as one who has relinquished your responsibility and shrunk back from your duty? He has given us an opportunity to serve Him in our generation. It is up to us to warn all of The Trend Toward Cultural Captivity. As we represent Him faithfully, he will use us as ambassadors who are effective and adequate as we make His Word known.

11. Being in the Arena

When the Apostle Paul was writing his Epistles to the Churches, and especially as he wrote the pastoral Epistles to Titus and Timothy, Cultural Captivity was an imminent possibility for all of the people. The politics of the day contributed to the erosion of values and principles. Christianity was abhorred by the civil and religious leaders of that day. To be identified with "The Way" was dangerous. Christians were being imprisoned, persecuted and being put to death. The death by stoning of Stephen in Acts 7 was only the Prelude to what would soon follow. In some of the last words penned by Paul, he was concerned that the younger Pastors would not be intimidated or surprised by the challenges that lay before them.

Paul wrote the following to Timothy, II Timothy 3:1-13 (NKJV Selected): "But know this, that in the last days perilous times will come: For men will be lovers of themselves, lovers of money, boasters, proud, blasphemers, disobedient to parents, unthankful, unholy, unloving, unforgiving, slanderers, without self-control, brutal, despisers of good, traitors, headstrong, haughty, lovers of pleasure rather than lovers of God, having a form of godliness but denying its power. And from such people turn away…these also resist the truth: men of corrupt minds, disapproved concerning the faith; but they will progress no further, for their folly will be manifest to all…But you have carefully followed my doctrine, manner of life, purpose, faith, long-suffering, love, perseverance, persecutions, afflictions, which happened to me…what persecutions I endured. And out of them all the Lord delivered me. Yes, and all who desire to live godly in Christ Jesus will suffer persecution. But evil men and impostors will grow worse and worse, deceiving and being deceived…" There are many who believe that "perilous times" are a growing reality in the world. The description of how people will be and behave seems as though it is a blueprint of and for the times in which we are living.

In the previous chapter there was notation from Ephesians 6:20 where Paul referred to himself as an "ambassador in chains." In the same passage (verse 11), Paul cites his personal experience of "persecutions and afflictions which happened to me." His use of the plural indicates that the persecutions and afflictions were ongoing and constant in his personal experience. There is a purpose in his mentioning these realities because he goes on to say (verse 12): "all who desire to live godly in Christ Jesus will suffer persecution." In the world today, there are many places where persecution is a reality. People are being imprisoned and killed because they believe in something other than Islam and Sharia Law.

In 1721-24, Isaac Watts was preparing a sermon based upon I Corinthians 16:13 (NKJV), "Be watchful, stand firm in the faith, act like men, be strong." He didn't have the MSG paraphrase available to him or he might have made use of the words recorded there (verses 13-14), "Keep your eyes open, hold tight to your convictions, give it all you've got, be resolute, and love without stopping." As Isaac Watts continued with his sermon preparation, words for a Hymn began to flow through his heart and mind. Some of the words are: "Am I a soldier of the cross, A follower of the Lamb, And shall I fear to own His cause, Or blush to speak His Name?" As he momentarily paused for reflection and thought about the magnitude of the task and the oftentimes dismal response to commitment to Christ and His cause, he penned the following words: "Must I be carried to the skies on flowery beds of ease, While others fought to win the prize, and sailed through bloody seas?" He clearly understood the things about which Paul was writing, especially "all who desire to live godly in Christ Jesus will suffer persecution." The same conditions would apply for all who would endeavor to serve faithfully. They should also expect to be chided, opposed, criticized, ostracized and persecuted. When the culture has eroded and collapsed, when all moral restraints have been jettisoned, one would do well to remember all those who have preceded us on this journey and path. Hebrews 11:35-38 (ESV) describes what many had to endure as they purposed to walk with Jesus Christ and to be an Ambassador for Him: "Some were tortured, refusing to accept release, so that they might rise again to a better life. Others suffered mocking and flogging, and even chains and imprisonment. They were stoned, they were sawn in two, they were killed with the sword. They went about in skins of sheep and goats, destitute, afflicted, mistreated, of whom the world was not worthy, wandering about in deserts and mountains, and in dens and caves of the earth."

Why were these descriptive words written in Hebrews 11? Was it intended as a reality check for the complacency of those days? Was it to redirect one's focus to the higher calling and purpose of God for His people and His Church? Almost immediately, a reason given follows in Hebrews 12:1-3 (ESV): "Therefore, since we are surrounded by so great a cloud of witnesses, let us also lay aside every weight, and sin which clings so closely, and let us run with endurance the race that is set before us, looking to Jesus, the founder and perfecter of our faith, who for the joy that was set before him endured the cross, despising the shame, and is seated at the right hand of the throne of God. Consider him who endured from sinners such hostility against himself, so that you may not grow weary or fainthearted." An emphasis should be placed on the words of verse 3: "Consider him who endured from sinners such hostility against himself." The words address the hostility and animosity of those who were opposed to Jesus Christ. They rejected His message and ministry. The purpose of Hebrews 11 is that we may learn from those who endured and suffered so much in previous generations. Their example should serve to encourage following generations too so that we will "run with endurance the race that is set before us." It also provides the example so that in our journey we "may not grow weary or fainthearted."

In June 2014, Franklin Graham wrote a column on "Praying For The Next Great Awakening." Part of what he shared included: "While doomsday appears to be knocking at our door, let me take you back to the early 1800s. Many think of it as "the good old days," but history tells us that society, even then, was as bad as it could get at that time. John Marshall, chief justice of the United States

Supreme Court, wrote to President James Madison and said, "The church is too far gone ever to be redeemed." When we examine why, we find that preachers had stopped preaching the whole Gospel of Jesus Christ, and the people were not hearing God's Word. What changed? Christians began to diligently pray for revival—and the result was the Second Great Awakening." These words are timely. The church and the world are so intertwined that it is difficult to differentiate one from the other. There is merit in the comments shared by Franklin Graham. There is also merit in the oft quoted words of Dietrich Bonhoeffer (1906-1945) who wrote a book about The Cost of Discipleship while in a Nazi prison cell. Just before the liberation, he was killed by the Nazis. The piercing words of contrast about discipleship that many repeat are: "Cheap grace is the deadly enemy of our Church. We are fighting today for costly grace…Grace is represented as the Church's inexhaustible treasury, from which it showers blessings with generous hands, without asking questions or fixing limits. Grace without price; grace without cost! The essence of grace, we suppose, is that the account has been paid in advance; and, because it has been paid, everything can be had for nothing…Cheap grace means grace as a doctrine, a principle, a system. It means forgiveness of sins proclaimed as a general truth, the love of God taught as the Christian 'conception' of God. An intellectual assent to that idea is held to be of itself sufficient to secure remission of sins…In such a Church the world finds a cheap covering for its sins; no contrition is required, still less any real desire to be delivered from sin. Cheap grace therefore amounts to a denial of the living Word of God, in fact, a denial of the Incarnation of the Word of God…Cheap grace is the preaching of forgiveness without requiring repentance, baptism without church discipline, Communion without confession…Cheap grace is grace without discipleship, grace without the cross, grace without Jesus Christ, living and incarnate." Does any of this sound familiar in terms of religion in our day? These words are descriptive of the state of the church today and the Trend Toward Cultural Captivity. It does not appear that we are too far removed from the actual Cultural Captivity taking place soon.

Bonhoeffer also shares his thoughts about Costly Grace. He wrote: "Costly grace is the treasure hidden in the field; for the sake of it a man will gladly go and sell all that he has. It is the pearl of great price...It is the kingly rule of Christ, for whose sake a man will pluck out the eye which causes him to stumble, it is the call of Jesus Christ at which the disciple leaves his nets and follows him. Costly grace is the gospel which must be sought...the gift which must be asked for, the door at which a man must knock. Such grace is costly because it calls us to follow, and it is grace because it calls us to follow Jesus Christ. It is costly because it costs a man his life, and it is grace because it gives a man the only true life. It is costly because it condemns sin, and grace because it justifies the sinner. Above all, it is costly because it cost God the life of his Son: you were bought at a price, and what has cost God much cannot be cheap for us. Above all, it is grace because God did not reckon his Son too dear a price to pay for our life, but delivered him up for us..."

Is this anywhere close to the message going out from the citadels of the traditional church? When people attend church today, is it a sober and reflective time as one thinks about this special time of being in the presence of God to worship Him along with those of like precious faith? Has worship become a time for frivolity and entertainment rather than seeking after the deep things of the whole counsel of God? When was the last time you can recall a sermon based upon a text such as Romans 11:29-36 (ESV)? The text reads: "For the gifts and the calling of God are irrevocable. For just as you were at one time disobedient to God but now have received mercy because of their disobedience, so they too have now been disobedient in order that by the mercy shown to you they also may now receive mercy. For God has consigned all to disobedience, that he may have mercy on all. Oh, the depth of the riches and wisdom and knowledge of God! How unsearchable are his judgments and how inscrutable his ways! For who has known the mind of the Lord, or who has been his counselor? Or who has given a gift to him that he might be repaid? For from him and through him and to him are all things. To him be glory forever. Amen." What does the text mean? How does it apply to my life today? What does it say to my world today? Why is it unheard today?

Bonhoeffer was on-target when he drew the distinctions between Cheap Grace and Costly Grace. He was measuring the Church during the uprising of World War II. If he was alive today, one can only imagine what his view of our culture and world would be. It would seem certain that his words would have as much sting today in terms of the embrace of Cheap Grace. He would doubtlessly herald the call for people to regain focus onto Costly Grace and why that should be what is embraced by the individual and the church. Continuing in the pathway of Cheap Grace will plunge one into Cultural Captivity. Being in the arena involves a choice and a commitment. Does that matter to you? What is your focus and commitment in terms of God's grace? Are you content to just get by with minimum application and call for commitment to follow Jesus Christ? What is your level of engagement in the task of reaching this generation with God's Word? What are you doing to counteract the trend toward cultural captivity?

12. A Possession Perspective

The idea of a safe environment and a desirable comfort zone is appealing to most people. We tend to like the Fairy Tale scenario where everyone lives happily ever after. The motivation and goal for life is to prepare for the future. The concept is to work now, save now, build now so the anticipated necessities for the future will have sufficient provision and a safety net. People do financial planning when they invest in Annuities and Tax Sheltered Accounts designed to supplement their Social Security Benefits when they retire from the workplace environment. Not too many are thinking in terms of a collapsing economy and the loss of one's possessions. The anticipation is for a peaceful existence that will be manageable and affordable.

As Jesus was preparing His disciples for their future and ministry task, He shared with them the response and reaction they can expect and will experience within a world and culture that has a different value system and standards. If Jesus was physically present in our country and culture, His message and comments would match that which He shared with His disciples. He might remind us of His words recorded in Matthew 6:31-34 (NIV): "So do not worry, saying, What shall we eat? or What shall we drink? or What shall we wear? For the pagans run after all these things, and your heavenly Father knows that you need them. But seek first His kingdom and His righteousness, and all these things will be given to you as well. Therefore do not worry about tomorrow, for tomorrow will worry about itself. Each day has enough trouble of its own." Jesus is setting a tone and parameters for His disciples who will be living out their lives in a hostile and dangerous environment. He is not saying one should not save for the future but He is saying that the future is so uncertain that the one's existing in that environment will require one to cling by faith to his Provider rather than clinging to temporal finances or investments. This idea is expressed in Luke 9:4 (NIV), He told them: "Take nothing for the journey, no staff, no bag, no bread, no money, no extra tunic." This is stated again in Luke 10:2-7 (NIV), He told them: "The harvest is plentiful, but the workers are few. Ask the Lord of the harvest, therefore, to send out workers into his harvest field. Go! I am sending you out like lambs among wolves. Do not take a purse or bag or sandals; and do not greet anyone on the road. When you enter a house, first say: Peace to this house. If a man of peace is there, your peace will rest on him; if not, it will return to you. Stay in that house, eating and drinking whatever they give you, for the worker deserves his wages. Do not move around from house to house." This principle is stated by Paul in Philippians 4:19, "And my God will meet all your needs according to his glorious riches in Christ Jesus." The Scripture is instructing the people of God that one's hope is not in things and the temporal but in faith and the adequate provision of the Lord for His followers.

    A Word of Caution: The teaching of Scripture in this regard is not suggesting that one should be careless and reckless with personal finances. A person is expected to be financially responsible in temporal matters. Three Scripture passages that should provide balance and perspective regarding finances are: (1) Deuteronomy 8:10-20 (NIV) - A Personal and National Understanding regarding finances and wealth: "When you have eaten and are satisfied, praise the Lord your God for the good land he has given you. Be careful that you do not forget the Lord your God, failing to observe his commands, his laws and his decrees that I am giving you this day. Otherwise, when you eat and are satisfied, when you build fine houses and settle down, and when your herds and flocks grow large and your silver and gold increase and all you have is multiplied, then your heart will become proud and you will forget the Lord your God, who brought you out of Egypt, out of the land of slavery...You may say to yourself: My power and the strength of my hands have produced this wealth for me. But remember the Lord your God, for it is he who gives you the ability to produce wealth, and so confirms his covenant, which he swore to your forefathers, as it is today. If you ever forget the Lord your God and follow other gods and worship and bow down to them, I testify against you today that you will surely be destroyed. Like the nations the Lord destroyed before you, so you will be destroyed for not obeying the Lord your God." In terms of The Trend Toward Cultural Captivity, does any of the above passage apply to this nation? How?

(2) A basic principle for life is given in Proverbs 22:17-28 (NIV Selected): "Pay attention and listen to the sayings of the wise; apply your heart to what I teach...So that your trust may be in the Lord...Do not exploit the poor because they are poor and do not crush the needy in court, for the Lord will take up their case and will plunder those who plunder them...Do not be a man who strikes hands in pledge or puts up security for debts; if you lack the means to pay, your very bed will be snatched from under you. Do not move an ancient boundary stone set up by your forefather." The teaching is to remind one of needed compassion and integrity in all matters and details of interactional life. It is clear that the Lord wants us to know that (a) He is observing what we do with our finances and in our treatment of others and (b) He is in control of what one has and can as easily and quickly remove it if an attitude and practice prevails where one is misusing that which the Lord has entrusted to His care and keeping.

(3) Proverbs 11:23-28 (NIV Selected): "The desire of the righteous ends only in good, but the hope of the wicked only in wrath. One man gives freely, yet gains even more; another withholds unduly, but comes to poverty. A generous man will prosper; he who refreshes others will himself be refreshed...He who seeks good finds goodwill, but evil comes to him who searches for it. Whoever trusts in his riches will fall, but the righteous will thrive like a green leaf." The lesson is that one should consider the merits of being generous rather than being miserly or stingy. None of the Biblical teaching suggests that one should be avant-garde (radical, unorthodox, reckless, daring) when it comes to responsible stewardship and the handling of possessions entrusted to one.

The tenth commandment given by God to His people states (Exodus 20:17, Deuteronomy 5:21, NIV): "You shall not covet your neighbor's wife. You shall not set your desire on your neighbor's house or land, his manservant or maidservant, his ox or donkey, or anything that belongs to your neighbor." A very clear directive issued by God about the need to abstain from coveting what others have and you may want. There is another implication to this commandment when Paul wrote in Colossians 3:5 (NKJV): "Therefore put to death your members which are on the earth: fornication, uncleanness, passion, evil desire, and covetousness, which is idolatry." Paul is bold to state that when one allows himself to covet someone else's possessions, it is equated with idolatry. This becomes even more serious because one has allowed the worship of things to supplant worship of God.

Two examples of greed and coveting after things of others are Achan in the Camp of Israel, and Ananias and Sapphire in the early church. While the situations are separated by hundreds of years, the negative result for a group of God's people would be impacted because of the actions of one or two people. Joshua 7:1-26 records how Joshua has led the people of God into The Promised Land and the victory at Jericho. This great triumph will be short-lived because very quickly they will experience a humiliating defeat. Three things that contribute to this defeat are: (a) self-confidence and sin, (b) carelessness regarding the devoted things ban, and (c) an individual's greed. This account is well known. Those who spied out Ai reported to Joshua that 3,000 men would be sufficient to attack and take possession of that city. They go in their own confidence and strength only to be met with opposition, pursuit and the death of some of their soldiers. Why did this happen? Joshua is concerned and prays to the Lord (Verses 7-9): "Alas, O Lord God, why have you brought this people over the Jordan at all, to give us into the hands of the Amorites, to destroy us? Would that we had been content to dwell beyond the Jordan! O Lord, what can I say, when Israel has turned their backs before their enemies! For the Canaanites and all the inhabitants of the land will hear of it and will surround us and cut off our name from the earth. And what will you do for your great name?"

One of the lessons Joshua and the people will need to learn is that sin cannot be overlooked or allowed to continue. The Lord's reply is very quick, concise and clear (Verses 10-12), "The Lord said to Joshua: Get up! Why have you fallen on your face? Israel has sinned; they have transgressed my covenant that I commanded them; they have taken some of the devoted things; they have stolen and lied and put them among their own belongings. Therefore the people of Israel cannot stand before their enemies. They turn their backs before their enemies, because they have become destined for destruction. I will be with you no more, unless you destroy the devoted things from among you." Joshua was not expecting to hear the words: "...they have become destined for destruction." For the people of God, Jericho had been placed under a ban regarding the devoted things. Technically, "The verb form, "haram", means: to ban, devote, or destroy utterly. There is to be an understanding and obedience that there must be an exclusion of an object from use or abuse by man along with its irreversible surrender to God." The ban is non-amendable and irrevocable. The principle is precise. Whatever God has forbidden we should not allow or permit. The directive of the Lord at this point is clear. Verse 13 is God's declaration of that which must be done: "Get up! Consecrate the people and say, Consecrate yourselves for tomorrow; for thus says the Lord, God of Israel: There are devoted things in your midst, O Israel. You cannot stand before your enemies until you take away the devoted things from among you."

The moment of truth takes place as Achan comes before Joshua and says (Verses 20-22): "Truly I have sinned against the Lord God of Israel, and this is what I did: when I saw...I coveted and took them. And see, they are hidden in the earth inside my tent..." The remainder of Joshua 7 describes what happened to Achan, his family, his possessions and the devoted things. They were taken away from the camp and were stoned and burned as a consequence of the greed and coveting of Achan.

Hundreds of years later, as the church was being formed and people were freely sharing what they had with others, Acts 5 records a similar incident to that found in Joshua 7. Acts 5:1-5 (NKJV) records: "But a certain man named Ananias, with Sapphire his wife, sold a possession. And he kept back part of the proceeds, his wife also being aware of it, and brought a certain part and laid it at the apostles' feet. But Peter said, Ananias, why has Satan filled your heart to lie to the Holy Spirit and keep back part of the price of the land for yourself? While it remained, was it not your own? And after it was sold, was it not in your own control? Why have you conceived this thing in your heart? You have not lied to men but to God. Then Ananias, hearing these words, fell down and breathed his last. So great fear came upon all those who heard these things." It is similar because this had become a matter of integrity regarding a gift that had been consecrated to God. Peter's rationale is fair and clear. Whatever Ananias had he could have kept but once he and Sapphira had agreed to give it all to the Lord they could no longer renegotiate the amount of the gift. When they withheld a portion for themselves, they had at that moment stolen from God. Just as Achan and his family died before the Lord the same would now be true for Ananias and Sapphira. The basic principle by which the Lord measures attitudes and commitments regarding what is given is established in Malachi 3:7-10. The blessings of God are promised and guaranteed for those who honor Him and His Word.

When avarice (insatiable greed for riches; inordinate, miserly desire to gain and hoard wealth) is present, God's commandments have been transgressed and His indignation will be made known. The desire to have more and more while giving less and less is part of the Trend Toward Cultural Captivity. A saying from the past that was intended to be humorous has become a sad reality and truism: "What's mine is mine and what's your's is mine." The welfare mentality of this day is becoming more and more the redistribution of wealth. Those who are working are supporting those who cannot find employment or those who are refusing to look for a job.

Some of the great Hymns of the past need to be part of today's awareness and consciousness. Hymns, such as: "All to Jesus, I surrender, All to Him I freely give...Worldly pleasures all forsaken...I surrender all." Another Hymn of this sort is: All for Jesus, All for Jesus...Let my hands perform His bidding, Let my feet run in His ways...Worldlings prize their gems of beauty, Cling to gilded toys of dust. Boast of wealth and fame and pleasure; Only Jesus will I trust...All for Jesus, All for Jesus..." Do these Hymns represent your consecration of all you are and have to Jesus Christ alone? Is this the message you share with those who are heading toward Cultural Captivity?

13. A Stewardship Perspective

The world will strive to fit one into it's mold. In a materialistic and commercialized society and culture, the goal is to impact lifestyle choices and behavior. If we allow these influences to infiltrate and alter our core values and foundational principles, we have exposure to and are in danger of cultural captivity. There is a way to avoid these things that seek to gain a foothold in our lives. There is an important principle contained in the words of a personal commitment shared by Jim Elliot (one of the five missionaries killed by the Auca Indians in Ecuador, 1956). In his Journal Entry for October 28, 1949, he wrote: "He is no fool who gives what he cannot keep to gain that which he cannot lose." He was referring to his sense of God's call and claim upon his life to serve the Lord Jesus Christ. His words should resonate with any serious-minded child of God. We are not to be content or satisfied with the enjoyment of where we are or what we have as valued possessions. There is a much greater and broader perspective that should be considered and pursued. Jim Elliot had the correct understanding of this perspective when he focused upon giving what you cannot keep and gaining what you cannot lose.

This chapter will seek to apply this principle of personal commitment to the area of our personal gains, possessions, assets and finances. This will not be a dissertation on the subject of Tithing. The argument that some are willing to make and adhere to states: "Tithing is an Old Testament concept. The tithe was a requirement of the Law in which the Israelites were to give 10 percent of the crops they grew and the livestock they raised to the tabernacle/temple (Leviticus 27:30, Numbers 18:26, Deuteronomy 14:24, 2 Chronicles 31:5). In fact, the Old Testament Law required multiple tithes: (a) one for the Levites, (b) one for the use of the temple and the feasts, and (c) one for the poor of the land (which would have pushed the total to around 23.3 percent). Some understand the Old Testament tithe as a method of taxation to provide for the needs of the priests and Levites in the sacrificial system."

With this being stated, one should also reference God's complaint against a non-compliant people in Malachi 1:6-14 (ASV). The indictment of the Lord is in terms of the heart motivation of the purpose in offering the gift to the Lord. The Lord is addressing the fact of the willingness to bring as an offering something considerably less than what is required and believing that will be acceptable. The Lord calls it profaning and polluting the table of the Lord. The Lord states His displeasure because of their deceitfulness and matter-of-factness before Him. In verse 13, a summary of God's complaint is: "You say also, Behold, what a weariness is it! and ye have sniffed at it, saith Jehovah of hosts; and you have brought that which was taken by violence, and the lame, and the sick; thus you bring the offering: should I accept this at your hand? saith Jehovah." The Lord is indicating that the heart attitude of the people bringing the sacrifices is repugnant to Him, as well as the gifts and sacrifices they thought He would receive.

The Lord's indictment continues in Malachi 3:7-10 with these words: "From the days of your fathers you have turned aside from My ordinances, and have not kept them. Return unto Me, and I will return unto you, says Jehovah of hosts. But you say, Wherein shall we return? Will a man rob God? Yet you rob me. But you say, Wherein have we robbed You? In tithes and offerings. You are cursed with the curse; for you rob Me, even this whole nation. Bring you the whole tithe into the store-house, that there may be food in My house, and prove Me now herewith, says Jehovah of hosts, if I will not open you the windows of heaven, and pour you out a blessing, that there shall not be room enough to receive it."

The principle is applied by the Lord for any of God's people in any generation. If one has any expectation of material blessing, it will be realized by those who respond proportionately with generous and joyous sacrifices to God. This type of response that honors God is stated in Hebrews 13:15-16, "Through him then let us offer up a sacrifice of praise to God continually, that is, the fruit of lips which make confession to his name. But to do good and to communicate forget not: for with such sacrifices God is well pleased." In a previous study, there was a discussion of the hortatory subjunctives, the "let us" phrases in the Book of Hebrews. The Hortatory Subjunctive is a statement urging others to join in some action. It is roughly the same as first person imperative, which does not exist in Greek. It is almost always translated "let us." By way of review, some examples of the Hortatory Scriptures are: Hebrews 10:22 , Let us come forward to the Holy of Holies with a true heart in full assurance of faith." Hebrews 12:1, "Let us run the race that is set before us." And, 1 John 4:7, "Beloved, let us love one another." The basic idea is that it is a directive of what all of us are to be doing regularly. Any modification or dilution of this directive is displeasing to the Lord and will result in the desired approval and blessing being withheld.

Our references to Old Testament tithing will only be in terms of concept, principle and purpose. We will be considering a discussion of proportionate giving from the abundance of that which God has entrusted to us. One of the things we should always remember about the Lord God is the statement in Psalm 84:11 (NKJV), "For the Lord God is a sun and shield; the Lord will give grace and glory; no good thing will He withhold from those who walk uprightly." The words of the Psalm and the words of the Lord in Malachi are concerned with the heart attitude of the individual regarding stewardship and giving to the Lord and the needs of others. The Amplified New Testament translates II Corinthians 9:7 with terms that are measuring the heart attitude of the one giving: "Let each one give as he has made up his own mind and purposed in his heart, not reluctantly or sorrowfully or under compulsion, for God loves (He takes pleasure in, prizes above other things, and is unwilling to abandon or to do without) a cheerful (joyous, prompt to do it) giver whose heart is in his giving."

What is a descriptive measure of a heart attitude that has escaped the thinking of a cultural captivity mindset? What has eluded them in terms of what pleasing to the Lord? The answer is given in II Corinthians 8:1-6 (NLT): "Now I want to tell you, dear brothers and sisters, what God in his kindness has done for the churches in Macedonia. Though they have been going through much trouble and hard times, their wonderful joy and deep poverty have overflowed in rich generosity. For I can testify that they gave not only what they could afford but far more. And they did it of their own free will. They begged us again and again for the gracious privilege of sharing in the gift for the Christians in Jerusalem. Best of all, they went beyond our highest hopes, for their first action was to dedicate themselves to the Lord and to us for whatever directions God might give them." The personal commitment was based upon who they were and what they had received as a provision from the hand of God. They were not grudging in their giving but generous, even to the point of giving beyond what they were able to give. The words of II Corinthians 9:7-9 (NLT) are instructive and encouraging: "You must each make up your own mind as to how much you should give. Don't give reluctantly or in response to pressure. For God loves the person who gives cheerfully. And God will generously provide all you need. Then you will always have everything you need and plenty left over to share with others. As the Scriptures say, Godly people give generously to the poor. Their good deeds will never be forgotten."

    David was referred to by the Lord in Acts 13:22, "I have found David the son of Jesse, a man after My heart, who shall do all My will." One example from the life of David that illustrates this truth is I Chronicles 29:9-21 in a prayer he offered before the people and the Lord: "Then the people rejoiced, for that they offered willingly, because with a perfect heart they offered willingly to Jehovah: and David the king also rejoiced with great joy. Wherefore David blessed Jehovah before all the assembly; and David said, Blessed be thou, O Jehovah, the God of Israel our father, for ever and ever. Thine, O Jehovah, is the greatness, and the power, and the glory, and the victory, and the majesty: for all that is in the heavens and in the earth [is thine]; thine is the kingdom, O Jehovah, and thou art exalted as head above all. Both riches and honor come of thee, and You rule over all; and in Your hand is power and might; and in Your hand it is to make great, and to give strength unto all. Now therefore, our God, we thank thee, and praise thy glorious name. But who am I, and what is my people, that we should be able to offer so willingly after this sort? For all things come of thee, and of thine own have we given thee. For we are strangers before thee, and sojourners, as all our fathers were: our days on the earth are as a shadow, and there is no abiding. O Jehovah our God, all this store that we have prepared to build thee a house for thy holy name cometh of thy hand, and is all thine own. I know also, my God, that You test the heart, and hast pleasure in uprightness. As for me, in the uprightness of my heart I have willingly offered all these things: and now have I seen with joy thy people, that are present here, offer willingly unto thee. O Jehovah, the God of Abraham, of Isaac, and of Israel, our fathers, keep this for ever in the imagination of the thoughts of the heart of thy people, and prepare their heart unto thee; and give unto Solomon my son a perfect heart, to keep thy commandments, thy testimonies, and thy statutes, and to do all these things, and to build the palace, for which I have made provision. And David said to all the assembly: Now bless Jehovah your God. And all the assembly blessed Jehovah, the God of their fathers, and bowed down their heads, and worshipped Jehovah, and the king. And they sacrificed sacrifices unto Jehovah, and offered burnt-offerings unto Jehovah, on the morrow after that day, even a thousand bullocks, a thousand rams, and a thousand lambs, with their drink-offerings, and sacrifices in abundance for all Israel."

    David and the people were enthusiastic and generous in all of what they gave and provided for the house of the Lord. They viewed it as a privilege and responded joyously. The heart attitude is measured by the Lord and one must be upright and committed to Him. The culture and society have a different measurement for attitude and benevolence. There are many secular organizations that do an acceptable benevolent work in communities, the nation and the world. The follower of Christ has an added dimension in life. There is a higher purpose and commitment that serves as the motivation of what one does and the levels of generosity. The child of God is not motivated to give in order to get something in return. The principle by which one lives is II Corinthians 9:6, "He that sows sparingly shall reap also sparingly; and he that sows bountifully shall reap also bountifully." This is a true and valid principle applicable for the totality of one's life. This is the way the Lord expects and wants His people to live in this culture. Anything short of that indicates one is drifting dangerously toward cultural captivity.

14. A Persecution Perspective

An important read and study is Hebrews 11. The context addresses the theme of "by faith" and how ordinary people were able to realize God's intervention in their lives in both unique and dynamic ways. The context also addresses the theme of persecution and how those experiencing hostility and adversity persevered amid the greatest pressures and severest conditions imaginable. Hebrews 11:38 contains this brief statement about those who were enduring persecution, "…of whom the world was not worthy."

In the Presbyterian Church in America devotional, This Day In Presbyterian History, is an entry for June 30, 2014 about the fiftieth anniversary celebration of the Korean Mission of the Presbyterian Church in the U.SA. In a paper by the Rev. Herbert E. Blair, he writes under the title of "Fifty Years of Development of the Korean Church." According to him, three main principles undergirded the PCUSA mission to Korea in the period between 1884-1934: (1) The supreme place given the Bible, with its simple Gospel message as the inspired, authoritative Word of God. (2) The common determination to make the Korean Church an indigenous church from the beginning, self-propagating, self-instructing, and self-governing. (3) A spirit of comity and cooperation." While this report seems to be positive and encouraging, there was another reality taking place. The paper continues, "But Blair also notes that there was great opposition to the gospel ministry in Korea in those days. Men were imprisoned and flogged and threatened with death for helping the foreigners bring in the Gospel. Terrible persecutions were inflicted by hostile communities or privately by families or by fathers and husbands. Young widows of the Church were snatched and sold by heathen relatives and terribly abused. Wives were beaten, dragged out of churches and through the streets by their hair and cursed, and their clothes hidden so that they could not go to church again. Some were locked up and food denied them. They were cast off for Christ's sake. Young boys suffered terrible beatings at the hands of brothers and fathers and were driven from home. Young girls were dragged away to heathen marriages and tortured if they protested. If they fled, they were arrested and forced back into weddings they could not escape." Persecution is an ongoing reality in many places in the world today. People are being imprisoned and put to death because they have placed their faith and trust in Jesus Christ. They are treated harshly and severely because they refuse to renounce their faith in Him. Jesus wanted His followers to be aware of opposition and hostility awaiting them if they identified themselves with Him and His message. An interesting statement made by Jesus is when He said to His disciples in John 15:17 (NKJV), "These things I command you, that you love one another." This word would be agreeable for all. The disciples could readily accept the challenge and potential of this command. It would make sense to be united and know the full ramifications of meaningful relationships and interaction. However, this statement is immediately followed by the hard and hate-filled times on their horizons. Jesus moved immediately to a more defining expectation and experience when He states, John 15:18-25 (NKJV), "If the world hates you, you know that it hated Me before it hated you. If you were of the world, the world would love its own. Yet because you are not of the world, but I chose you out of the world, therefore the world hates you. Remember the word that I said to you: A servant is not greater than his master. If they persecuted Me, they will also persecute you. If they kept My word, they will keep yours also. But all these things they will do to you for My name's sake, because they do not know Him who sent Me. If I had not come and spoken to them, they would have no sin, but now they have no excuse for their sin. He who hates Me hates My Father also. If I had not done among them the works which no one else did, they would have no sin; but now they have seen and also hated both Me and My Father. But this happened that the word might be fulfilled which is written in their law: They hated Me without a cause." In the context the word Jesus uses to emphasize their hatred of Him means, "has hated and still hates." It is a determination of their will and a mindset to hate Jesus, hate what he said and does, and hate anyone who follows Him and adheres to His teaching. Hatred carries with it the meaning of intense dislike, or extreme aversion and hostility. Synonyms include the idea of animosity, loathing and abomination. Jesus is underscoring for His followers the intense disdain they will have to experience and endure if they are His followers.

Jesus also shares with them that they can expect and will experience the breakdown of normal and natural relationships, betrayal, arrest, inconvenience, flogging, hatred, persecution and homelessness. At such times, it will serve as an opportunity to be witnesses for and about Him before all sorts of people. In Matthew 10:16-26 (NIV) Jesus is speaking and says, "I am sending you out like sheep among wolves. Therefore be as shrewd as snakes and as innocent as doves. Be on your guard against men; they will hand you over to the local councils and flog you in their synagogues. On my account you will be brought before governors and kings as witnesses to them and to the Gentiles. But when they arrest you, do not worry about what to say or how to say it. At that time you will be given what to say, for it will not be you speaking, but the Spirit of your Father speaking through you. Brother will betray brother to death, and a father his child; children will rebel against their parents and have them put to death. All men will hate you because of me, but he who stands firm to the end will be saved. When you are persecuted in one place, flee to another. I tell you the truth, you will not finish going through the cities of Israel before the Son of Man comes. A student is not above his teacher, nor a servant above his master. It is enough for the student to be like his teacher, and the servant like his master. If the head of the house has been called Beelzebub, how much more the members of his household! So do not be afraid of them."

A primary reason for their vehement hatred of Jesus Christ relates directly to Who He is and what He claims to be. The opposition had discerned that Jesus was claiming to be God. Just one illustration in this area are the references to the Creation of the world and universe. It is clear in Genesis 1 that, "In the beginning, God" created all things. This was fine until John wrote in John 1,

"In the beginning was the Word, and the Word was with God and the Word was God. All things were made by Him and without Him was not anything made that was made." If clarity is needed in terms of the reference to "Him" in a creative narrative, there is clarification given in Colossians 1:13-18 (NKJV): "He has delivered us from the power of darkness and conveyed us into the kingdom of the Son of His love, in whom we have redemption through His blood, the forgiveness of sins. He is the image of the invisible God, the firstborn over all creation. For by Him all things were created that are in heaven and that are on earth, visible and invisible, whether thrones or dominions or principalities or powers. All things were created through Him and for Him. And He is before all things, and in Him all things consist. And He is the head of the body, the church, who is the beginning, the firstborn from the dead, that in all things He may have the preeminence." Another passage to note is Hebrews 1:1-3 (NKJV), "God, who at various times and in various ways spoke in time past to the fathers by the prophets, has in these last days spoken to us by His Son, whom He has appointed heir of all things, through whom also He made the worlds; who being the brightness of His glory and the express image of His person, and upholding all things by the word of His power, when He had by Himself purged our sins, sat down at the right hand of the Majesty on high…"

There are other areas and claims of Jesus that caused the hostility of those rejecting Him. In a confrontational exchange, John 8:37-45 (NKJV), Jesus stated the following: "I know that you are Abraham's descendants, but you seek to kill Me, because My word has no place in you. I speak what I have seen with My Father, and you do what you have seen with your father. They answered and said to Him: Abraham is our father. Jesus said to them: If you were Abraham's children, you would do the works of Abraham. But now you seek to kill Me, a Man who has told you the truth which I heard from God. Abraham did not do this. You do the deeds of your father…If God were your Father, you would love Me, for I proceeded forth and came from God; nor have I come of Myself, but He sent Me. Why do you not understand My speech? Because you are not able to listen to My word. You are of your father the devil, and the desires of your father you want to do. He was a murderer from the beginning, and does not stand in the truth, because there is no truth in him. When he speaks a lie, he speaks from his own resources, for he is a liar and the father of it. But because I tell the truth, you do not believe Me." The situation escalates to a point where those who are hostile to Jesus Christ decided the best action and result would be to stone Him to death.

The narrative of John 8:54-59 (NKJV) indicates the level of the rejection and hostility. The passage indicates: "Jesus answered: If I honor Myself, My honor is nothing. It is My Father who honors Me, of whom you say that He is your God. Yet you have not known Him, but I know Him. And if I say: I do not know Him, I shall be a liar like you; but I do know Him and keep His word. Your father Abraham rejoiced to see My day, and he saw it and was glad. Then the Jews said to Him: You are not yet fifty years old, and have You seen Abraham? Jesus said to them: Most assuredly, I say to you, before Abraham was, I AM. Then they took up stones to throw at Him; but Jesus hid Himself and went out of the temple, going through the midst of them, and so passed by." His claim to be "I AM" is viewed as blasphemy by those hostile to Him. "I AM" is the unique identity of Jehovah God (see further explanation of this in Chapter 2). When Jesus was claiming identity with "I AM", in John 10:9-11 he states: "I AM the door; by me if any man enter in, he shall be saved…" He also goes on to state: "I AM the good shepherd: the good shepherd lays down his life for the sheep." His opponents understood that Jesus Christ is claiming to be God, Messiah and Redeemer. These declarations of fact infuriated the religious leaders and those who attended the Synagogue for their religious tradition and ritualistic observations.

Jesus was very clear about the opposition He would face and the persecution that His followers would be called upon to endure. In the Beatitudes, Matthew 5:10-12 (ESV), Jesus stated: "Blessed are those who are persecuted for righteousness' sake, for theirs is the kingdom of heaven. Blessed are you when others revile you and persecute you and utter all kinds of evil against you falsely on my account. Rejoice and be glad, for your reward is great in heaven, for so they persecuted the prophets who were before you." Three times the word "persecute" is stated in terms of it being "blessed" experience and identity. While Wikipedia fails to recognize religious persecution as a current concern, their definition of persecution includes the following: "Persecution is the systematic mistreatment of an individual or group by another individual or group. The most common forms are religious persecution, ethnic persecution and political persecution although there is naturally some overlap between these terms. The inflicting of suffering, harassment, isolation, imprisonment, fear, or pain are all factors that may establish persecution. Even so, not all suffering will necessarily establish persecution. The suffering experienced by the victim must be sufficiently severe. The threshold level of severity has been a source of much debate." Wikipedia also states the following: "Religious persecution is a systematic mistreatment of an individual or group due to their religious affiliation. Not only theorists of secularization (who presume a decline of religiousity in general) would willingly assume that religious persecution is a thing of the past. However, with the rise of fundamentalism this assumption has become even more controversial. Indeed, in many countries of the world today, religious persecution is a Human Rights problem…The persecution of Christians is religious persecution that Christians sometimes undergo as a consequence of professing their faith, both historically and in the current era. In the two thousand years of the Christian faith, about 70 million believers have been killed for their faith, of whom 45.5 million or 65% were in the twentieth century…200 million Christians are vulnerable to persecution in the world, especially in war-torn Iraq and other Middle-Eastern countries and parts of Asia." Obviously, persecution extends in other places and in other forms and intensity.

    The Religion News Service reported on July 28th, 2014, "Secretary of State John Kerry announced that Turkmenistan has joined the State Department's list of worst religious freedom offenders. The State Department's 'Countries of Particular Concern' list had remained static since 2006, when eight countries - Burma, China, Eritrea, Iran, North Korea, Saudi Arabia, Sudan and Uzbekistan - were designated as CPC (Countries of Particular Concern). The report summary also names Syria, Sri Lanka, Egypt, Iraq, Bangladesh, Indonesia, India and Nigeria for failing to protect vulnerable religious communities, which often face violence, discrimination and harassment. During August and September, ISIS (Islamic State In Syria) became a reality and their radicalism has included beheading people, burying some alive and shooting others. In 2013, the world witnessed the largest displacement of religious communities in recent memory. In almost every corner of the globe, millions of Christians, Muslims, Hindus, and others representing a range of faiths were forced from their homes on account of their religious beliefs. Communities are disappearing from their traditional and historic homes and dispersing across the geographic map. In conflict zones, in particular, this mass displacement has become a pernicious norm."

Elsewhere in the world, Newsweek Magazine reported: "The mob howled for vengeance, the missiles raining down on the synagogue walls as the worshippers huddled inside. It was a scene from Europe in the 1930s, except this was eastern Paris on the evening of July 13, 2014. Thousands had gathered to demonstrate against the Israeli bombardment of Gaza. But the protest soon turned violent and against Jews in general. One of those trapped told Israeli television that the streets outside were 'like an intifada' - the Palestinian uprising against Israeli occupation. Some of the trapped Jews fought their way out as the riot police dispersed the crowd. Two weeks later, 400 protesters attacked a synagogue and Jewish-owned businesses in Sarcelles, in the north of Paris, shouting 'Death to the Jews.' France has suffered the worst violence, but anti-Semitism is spiking across Europe, fueled by the war in Gaza. In Britain, the Community Security Trust (CST) says there were around 100 anti-Semitic incidents in July, double the usual number. The CST has issued a security alert for Jewish institutions. In Berlin a crowd of anti-Israel protesters had to be prevented from attacking a synagogue. In Liege, Belgium, a café owner put up a sign saying dogs were welcome, but Jews were not allowed." Demonstrations against the Jews have also taken place in Canada, New York City and Boston.

The Christian communities throughout the world may be lulled into thinking they are exempt from anti-Christian violence and protest. That is a false concept and belief. If the Church is being the Church Jesus Christ wants it to be, there will be protests, opposition and persecution. One need only look at the ministry of Jesus Christ when He walked upon the earth. He knew what opposition, threats and hostility was toward Him. He prepared His followers for similar opposition and persecution if they followed Him wholeheartedly. A summary about the animosity toward Jesus Christ appear in His own words as recorded in John 5:16-18, "And this was why the Jews were persecuting Jesus, because he was doing these things on the Sabbath. But Jesus answered them: My Father is working until now, and I am working. This was why the Jews were seeking all the more to kill him, because not only was he breaking the Sabbath, but he was even calling God his own Father, making himself equal with God."

If we are to represent Him in this world, nation, culture and society, the words of Jesus recorded in John 15:20 (ESV) echo down to us today, "Remember the word that I said to you: A servant is not greater than his master. If they persecuted me, they will also persecute you." If you stand in the gap and seek to persuade those who are caught in the trend toward cultural captivity, you will be despised and become the recipient of oppression and persecution. May the words of Hebrews 11:38 be said of us or written as our epitaph: "Of whom the world was not worthy."

15. Getting the Gears to Mesh

The earliest automobiles manufactured came with a Standard Transmission. This meant that a person had to learn and exercise coordination skills, such as (1) press down on a clutch pedal, (2) use a shift handle to select the appropriate gear (first gear if you were not yet moving; second gear for increased acceleration; and third gear once a desired cruising sped was achieved) and (3) press the accelerator slowly as the clutch was being let up so that the result would be a smooth motion. Until those skills were attained, one might experience a hopping and bucking effect if the clutch was let up too quickly without adequate and necessary acceleration. If the clutch was not depressed when shifting into a desired gear, there would be a crunching and grinding sound because the gears were unable to mesh appropriately.

In the twenty-first century, we are way beyond the old mechanical technology of the nineteenth and twentieth centuries. The advances in electronics and technology are incredible and amaze the person of normal/average intelligence. Despite the technological advances, these things have not prevented the trend toward cultural captivity. In the process of our advances, there has also been a departure from foundational principles and core values that determined and defined our society and culture. It modeled an adherence to the Judeo-Christian principles and concepts. Today it is a time of departure from the significant core values of earlier days. Have we allowed ourselves to become so sophisticated and advanced that we no longer realize or sense the need for these foundational truths? As we stand amid the trend toward cultural captivity we identify with the words of David in Psalm 11:3, "if the foundations are destroyed, what can the righteous do?" Why is it that so few people are concerned? Where is the heart-cry emanating from the church in behalf of the souls of people? Are we no longer sensitive to the needs of lost souls? Have our consciences become seared to a point where we are scarred and calloused toward the lost?

This reminds one of a story written by Amy Carmichael in 1890 representing her concern for the lost souls of India. She wrote about a dream and vision she had of the lost and perishing. The title of her writing was, Things As They Are. Part of what she wrote included the following: "The tom-toms thumped straight on through the night, and the darkness shuddered round me like a living, feeling thing. I could not go to sleep, so I lay awake and looked and I saw as it seemed, this: That I stood on a grassy hill and at my feet a precipice broke sheer down into infinite space. I looked but saw no bottom--only cloud shapes, black and furiously coiled; and great shadowed, shrouded hollows and unfathomable depths. Back I drew, dizzy at the depth. Then I saw forms of people moving single file along the grassy hill. They were making for the edge. There was woman with a baby in her arms and another little child holding onto her dress; she was on the very verge. Then I saw that she was blind. She lifted her foot for the next step, She was over and the children over with her. Oh, the cry as they went over. Then I saw more streams of people flowing from all quarters--all were blind, stone blind. All made straight for the precipice edge. There were shrieks, as they suddenly knew themselves falling and a tossing up of helpless arms catching, clutching at empty air. But some went over quietly and fell without a sound. Then I wondered, with a wonder that was simply agony, why no one stopped them at the edge. I could not. I was glued to the ground. And I could not call; though I strained and tried only a whisper would come. Then I saw that along the edge there were sentries set at intervals, but the intervals were far too great. There were great wide unguarded gaps between and over these gaps the people fell in their blindness quite unwarned. And the green grass seemed blood red to me and the gulf yawned like the mouth of hell."

She mentions some who could've made a difference but they were preoccupied with the trivial. Her words are: "Then I saw, like a little picture of peace, a group of people under some trees with their backs turned towards the gulf. They were making daisy chains. Sometimes when a piercing shriek cut the quiet air and reached them, it disturbed them and they thought it a rather vulgar noise. And if one of their numbers started up and wanted to go do something to help, then all the others would pull that one down. Why should you get so excited about it? You must wait for a definite call to go. You haven't finished your daisy chains yet. It would be really selfish, they said, to leave us to finish the work alone. There was another group. It was made up of people whose great desire was to get more sentries out. But they found that very few wanted to go, and sometimes there were no sentries set for miles and miles of the edge. Once a girl stood alone in her place waving the people back; but her mother and other relations called, reminded her that her furlough was due. She must not break the rules. And being tired and needing a change, she had to go and rest for a while. But no one was sent to guard her gap, and over and over the people fell like a waterfall of souls. Once a child caught at a tuft of grass that grew at the very brink of the gulf. It clung convulsively and it called, but nobody seemed to hear. Then the roots of the grass gave way and with a cry the child went over, its two little hands still holding tight to the torn-off bunch of grass. And the girl who longed to be back at her gap thought she heard the little one cry. She sprang up and wanted to go, at which they reproved her reminding her that no one is necessary anywhere." Is that where we are today in the church? Are we all organization but devoid of a sense of mission? Have we forgotten the coordination necessary in getting the gears to mesh? Are we ignoring the grinding gears? Have we become indifferent to the plight of the lost and perishing? Do we care about those who have approached the edge of the precipice? Should our voice cry out warning of the immediacy of the peril that is imminent?

    The church at large has become more and more diverse. There is polarization and paralysis that prevents the church from coming anywhere close to where The Head of the Church desires it to be. The message of the church has become diluted and the mission of the church has become derailed. It's almost as though a satanic force was at work and the devil was the engineer of a train that is accelerating as it races toward doom and peril. An old expression says: "Don't throw the wrench into the works/gears." The basic meaning of that expression is defined as follows: "In the beginning of the Industrial Revolution, people were being replaced by machines, so they would try to harm the machines by throwing things into the gearboxes. In Belgium, they would throw their wooden shoes into the gears. The Flemish and French word for shoe is "sabot." When the workers threw their shoes into machines, they were sabotaging them." A wrench in the works or gears is also seen as being: "a nuisance, something that distracts from getting things done." This can be an apt assessment of churches today and why their influence has been waning. It is a lack of vision and mission that has disrupted how the church should function and where it should be going. Jeremiah 5:30-31 (NKJV) indicates conditions that prevailed in the day of the prophet: "An astonishing and horrible thing Has been committed in the land: The prophets prophesy falsely, and the priests rule by their own power; and My people love to have it so. But what will you do in the end?" Can we begin to sense and imagine a people believing that which is false and completely contrary to the way and will of the sovereign God?

The question was posed by the prophet: "But what will you do in the end?" How would you answer that question today? Do those words apply in any way for the contemporary church and how it portrays itself in the world, nation, culture and society? The Scriptures indicate that a day is coming when I Thessalonians 2:3-12 (NIV) will be the reality. The text indicates: "Don't let anyone deceive you in any way, for that day will not come until the rebellion occurs and the man of lawlessness is revealed, the man doomed to destruction. He will oppose and will exalt himself over everything that is called God or is worshiped, so that he sets himself up in God's temple, proclaiming himself to be God. Don't you remember that when I was with you I used to tell you these things? And now you know what is holding him back, so that he may be revealed at the proper time. For the secret power of lawlessness is already at work; but the one who now holds it back will continue to do so till he is taken out of the way. And then the lawless one will be revealed, whom the Lord Jesus will overthrow with the breath of his mouth and destroy by the splendor of his coming. The coming of the lawless one will be in accordance with the work of Satan displayed in all kinds of counterfeit miracles, signs and wonders, and in every sort of evil that deceives those who are perishing. They perish because they refused to love the truth and so be saved. For this reason God sends them a powerful delusion so that they will believe the lie and so that all will be condemned who have not believed the truth but have delighted in wickedness." Have we arrived at that place in the world? Are we running out of time to both be and make a difference for Jesus Christ? What can you do for Him today? What will you do for Him?

Amy Carmichael concluded her manuscript with these words: "The tom-toms still beat heavily. The darkness still shuddered and shivered about me. I heard the yells of the devil dancers and the weird, wild shriek of the devil-possessed just outside the gate. What does it matter after all? It has gone on for years. It will go on for years. I make such a fuss about it. God forgive us. God arouse us. Shame us out of our callousness, shame us out of our sin. Talking of this dream that she had, of the people falling over the cliff and no one paying any attention--it was very difficult for her to get people back in England to take any action." Have we now become a person of interest in the account written by Amy Carmichael? Has indifference, apathy and callousness impacted our personal vision and level of compassion for the lost? Are we so preoccupied with ourselves and our self-interests that the issue of souls plunging over the precipice into a bottomless abyss is of no concern to us? How do you believe The Head of The Church views all of this? How does He view you? What would be the right and wise choice for us to make? Is there a gap anywhere that you can stand in and any effort that you can exert in the effort of warning souls who are headed for disaster, peril and certain death?

Hebrews 13:16-17 (NLT) references the subject of those who look after and are concerned for the souls of others. The verses state: "Don't forget to do good and to share what you have with those in need, for such sacrifices are very pleasing to God. Obey your spiritual leaders and do what they say. Their work is to watch over your souls, and they know they are accountable to God. Give them reason to do this joyfully and not with sorrow. That would certainly not be for your benefit." The direct application of these words is in reference to church leaders fulfilling a responsibility for those under their spiritual care. Their duty is (1) to watch over your souls, (2) they are accountable to God, and (3) their care is for your benefit. By extension, in terms of the lost, the principle is the same. Our task commissioned by Jesus Christ is to focus on the lost souls throughout the world. We should focus on those approaching the precipice of the great gulf.

Jude 1:20-23 (NIV) emphasizes the extent and intensity of our effort to reach lost souls. Jude records these words: "But you, dear friends, build yourselves up in your most holy faith and pray in the Holy Spirit. Keep yourselves in God's love as you wait for the mercy of our Lord Jesus Christ to bring you to eternal life. Be merciful to those who doubt; snatch others from the fire and save them; to others show mercy, mixed with fear--hating even the clothing stained by corrupted flesh." If this was our focus and passion, we would risk reaching over the edge of the abyss to prevent souls from falling and perishing. There are many who are caught in the trend toward cultural captivity. They might even be active and willing to throw a wrench into the gears to prevent us from reaching them. Even if that is the case, by whatever means and effort required, we should exert ourselves and try to reach them if we can. Even if we should fail, we will have the satisfaction of having tried our best to reach the most souls with the message of hope and deliverance in the Lord Jesus Christ. This is the message that can prevent some from becoming a part of the trend toward cultural captivity.

16. Missing Ingredients

If you were a baker in charge of making bread, your skill and expertise would be gauged by the recipe you utilized. You would not be a credible baker if you disregarded the needed and necessary ingredients for making an edible loaf of bread. If you were a flippant or matter-of-fact baker, you might mix your idea of necessary ingredients randomly. In doing so, you might carelessly omit an ingredient or two and your result would be less than adequate. Without yeast, the bread will not rise. Without sugar and salt, the bread will be distasteful. Without oil or butter, the ingredients will not blend correctly. It might cause those who tasted your randomly mixed bread to seek a different baker who was more careful and consistent in how he approached his craft. Those who desired a good and tasty loaf of bread would be disappointed and seek satisfaction elsewhere.

In considering the Trend Toward Cultural Captivity, one of the contributing factors for this trend is the ineffectiveness and tastelessness of the church. Within the church, there are several missing ingredients. One missing ingredient is people. Those who study statistics have noted the steady decline in church attendance and membership. Additionally, those churches where there has been no decline also indicate there has been no growth. The church attendance has become static and some would add it has also become stagnant. *The Huffington Post*, October 2013, had a presentation submitted by Steve McSwain on the state of the church in the nation. Some of what was published indicated: "Between the years 2010 and 2012, more than half of all churches in America added not one new member. Each year, nearly 3 million more previous churchgoers enter the ranks of the religiously unaffiliated." Part of the report focused on at least "Seven Trends Impacting Church Decline." The list included the following: (1) The demographic remapping of American Whites indicates they are the majority today at 64 percent. In 30 to 40 years, they will be the minority...Furthermore, America is aging... (2) Technology is changing everything we do, including how we do church...Instead of embracing the technology and adapting their worship experiences to include the technology, scores of traditional churches, mainline Protestant, and almost all Catholic churches do not utilize the very instruments that, without which, few Millennials would know how to communicate or interact. (3) Leadership Crisis: Clergy abuse, the cover-up by the Church, and fundamentalist preachers and congregations have been driving people away from the Church, and continue to drive people away, faster than any other causes combined. (4) Competition: People have more choices on weekends than simply going to church. Ed Stetzer of Christianity Today has three different categories of Christians: First, there are cultural Christians or those who believe themselves to be Christians simply because their culture says they are. Second, there are congregational Christians who are loosely connected to the church. Third, there are the convictional Christians. These are the true Christians who are actually living their faith. (5) Religious Pluralism: People have more choices today...The fact is, people today meet other people of entirely different faith traditions and, if they are discovering anything at all, it is that there are scores of people who live as much, if not more, like Christ than many of the Christians they used to sit beside in church. (6) The Contemporary Worship Experience: It's been the trend in the last couple of decades for traditional, mainline churches to pretend to be something they're not. (7) Phony Advertising: You cannot tell the Millennials that your church welcomes everybody -- that all can come to Jesus -- and then, when they come, what they find are few mixed races or no mixed couples. You cannot say: Everybody is welcome here if, by that, you really mean, so long as you're like the rest of us, straight and in a traditional family."

    Several years ago, I was excited to be invited to a church as a possible candidate to be the Pastor of the church. We drove to the city and deliberately arrived earlier than the suggested hour. Our plan was to drive through the area to see the community and what was taking place in homes nearby to the church. There was busy activity in the driveways and yards of various homes. It soon became obvious that the activity was not preparation for driving to a church for Sunday School and a Worship Service. Different families were indicating that Sunday was their day for their planned activity and not The Lord's Day and His desire to have a people who would worship Him in spirit and in truth. The interview at the church inquired about my view of church numeric growth. Believing that it was a moment for candor and forthrightness, I told about our driving through the neighborhood and observing the activity around various homes. I asked them if they had ever done so themselves and what level of outreach they had previously had in their community and near neighbors. Do I need to supply you with their response? Can you determine what it was? If I asked your church that question, how would it respond? How would you respond? In case you're wondering, their response was an uncomfortable (and embarrassed) negative. Just as an aside, do you think they followed up with me to pursue Pastoral possibilities in and for that church and area? Try and echo a negative and you have given the correct response. There was a lack of vision and sense of mission. If they were uncomfortable and embarrassed by my question, what will they be when Jesus begins His process of separating the sheep from the goats in Matthew 25:31-46. His inferred questions regarding the hungry, thirsty, naked, strangers, sick and imprisoned cause a question to be asked: "Lord, when did we see you" in any of these circumstances? His declaration to them is: "Truly, I say to you, as you did not do it to one of the least of these, you did not do it to me." Would that cause discomfort and embarrassment for the inquirer? Yes! More importantly, what is the designated end for those who were negligent in these areas? Verse 46 supplies the answer: "And these will go away into eternal punishment, but the righteous into eternal life." Is that a hard truth to consider? One thing that is often forgotten in church life is that each one needs to be committed to taking a serious God seriously. If one feels the discomfort now when considering the hard truth, how do you suppose one will feel when Jesus is doing the separating based on His criteria for ministry?

Another missing ingredient in the church today is a sound biblical teaching and preaching ministry. If a guest was invited to dinner in your home, they would have an expectation of a well-prepared meal. The presentation of the meal when served would indicate the care and preparation that was an important factor for the one who planned the meal. In other words, the meal about to be revealed would indicate careful planning, diligent preparation and appealing presentation. In I Peter 5:2 (KJV) the instruction is: "Feed the flock of God which is among you, taking the oversight thereof, not by constraint, but willingly; not for filthy lucre, but of a ready mind." When did Peter learn this principle and duty to "feed and tend" God's flock? In John 21:15-17 (NIV), Jesus has focused upon Peter and the level of love he has for Him. Jesus was emphasizing with Peter that failure is not final. There is always an opportunity for recovery and renewal. In this exchange, there are three identical directives given to Peter. The verses state: "When they had finished eating, Jesus said to Simon Peter: Simon son of John, do you truly love me more than these? Yes, Lord, he said, you know that I love you. Jesus said: Feed my lambs. Again Jesus said: Simon son of John, do you truly love me? He answered, Yes, Lord, you know that I love you. Jesus said: Take care of my sheep. The third time he said to him: Simon son of John, do you love me?" Peter was hurt because Jesus asked him the third time, "Do you love me? He said, Lord, you know all things; you know that I love you. Jesus said: Feed my sheep." The direction is clearly stated: Feed and take care of My lambs and sheep. There is no acceptable excuse for the lack of care for the lambs and sheep.

To feed and take care of the lambs and sheep will require planning and preparation. When Paul was saying his farewell, we read in Acts 20:18-27 NKJV) his assessment of his ministry with and among them. Paul said: "You know, from the first day that I came to Asia, in what manner I always lived among you, serving the Lord with all humility, with many tears and trials which happened to me by the plotting of the Jews; how I kept back nothing that was helpful, but proclaimed it to you, and taught you publicly and from house to house, testifying to Jews, and also to Greeks, repentance toward God and faith toward our Lord Jesus Christ. And see, now I go bound in the spirit to Jerusalem, not knowing the things that will happen to me there, except that the Holy Spirit testifies in every city, saying that chains and tribulations await me. But none of these things move me; nor do I count my life dear to myself, so that I may finish my race with joy, and the ministry which I received from the Lord Jesus, to testify to the gospel of the grace of God. And indeed, now I know that you all, among whom I have gone preaching the kingdom of God, will see my face no more. Therefore I testify to you this day that I am innocent of the blood of all men. For I have not shunned to declare to you the whole counsel of God." Paul indicates the correlation of one's life and how it is to be consistently lived, and the preaching/teaching and how it is to be systematically and thoroughly prepared and proclaimed. This concept is amplified in Jude 1:3 (NKJV), "Beloved, while I was very diligent to write to you concerning our common salvation, I found it necessary to write to you exhorting you to contend earnestly for the faith which was once for all delivered to the saints."

In religious parlance (manner of speaking), this type of ministry practice would be in the area of systematic theology and apologetics. CARM (Christian Apologetics and Research Ministry) gives the basic idea and meaning of apologetics: "The word apologetics is derived from the Greek word *apologia* which means to make a defense. It has come to mean a viable and logical defense of the faith. Apologetics covers many areas: who Jesus is, the reliability of the Bible, refuting cults, Biblical evidences in history and archeology, answering objections, etc. In short, it deals with giving reasons for Christianity being the true religion. We are called by God to give an *apologia*, a defense: (I Peter 3:15) "but sanctify Christ as Lord in your hearts, always being ready to make a defense to everyone who asks you to give an account for the hope that is in you, yet with gentleness and reverence." A major missing ingredient in the church today is in the area of systematic theology and apologetics.

James Perry

CARM has stated a good order of subjects beginning with Jesus. If religious practice and exercise is to have any validity to it at all, it must begin with Jesus Christ. A good starting point in one's apologetic about Jesus is I Peter 1:18-21, "knowing that you were redeemed, not with corruptible things, with silver or gold, from your vain manner of life handed down from your fathers; but with the precious blood, as of a lamb without spot, even the blood of Christ: who was foreknown indeed before the foundation of the world, but was manifested at the end of times for your sake, who through him are believers in God, that raised him from the dead, and gave him glory; so that your faith and hope might be in God." This is a truth that is foundational in other Scriptures about the work and provision of Jesus Christ. Ephesians 1:7, "in whom we have our redemption through his blood, the forgiveness of our trespasses (sins), according to the riches of his grace," and Colossians 1:13-14, "who delivered us out of the power of darkness, and translated us into the kingdom of the Son of his love; in whom we have our redemption, the forgiveness of our sins…" This truth is also emphasized in I Corinthians 15:1-4, "Now I make known unto you brethren, the gospel which I preached unto you, which also ye received, wherein also ye stand, by which also ye are saved…For I delivered unto you first of all that which also I received: that Christ died for our sins according to the Scriptures; and that he was buried; and that he hath been raised on the third day according to the Scriptures…" Additionally, II Corinthians 5:14-21, part of which states: "For the love of Christ constrains us; because…one died for all…and he died for all, that they that live should no longer live unto themselves, but unto him who for their sakes died and rose again…Wherefore if any man is in Christ, he is a new creature: the old things are passed away; behold, they are become new…Him who knew no sin he made to be sin on our behalf; that we might become the righteousness of God in him."

Volumes could be written on the above verses about Jesus Christ, redemption, His blood, forgiveness of sins, new creature in Christ, righteousness of God in us, etc. A pastor, a shepherd of God's flock who is to declare the whole counsel of God, should be a theologian (a specialist in God's Words). The task of a shepherd is to provide his flock with the most nourishing food for the growth and development of the sheep and lambs. If he takes the flock into the weeds and briers, they will become malnourished, weak and sickly. As Jesus said to Peter (John 21), the servant of the Lord is to feed the lambs, take care of the flock and feed the sheep. Anything less than that is disobedience and failure. He is to be a pastor and apologist for the flock for which he has responsibility. If any of the apologetic ingredients are missing in a church ministry, the result will be something that is tasteless and of little value.

As I was finishing this chapter, the monthly letter from The Navigators for July 1, 2014 arrived. The lead article by Doug Nuenke, U. S. President of Navigators, is entitled: "Changing Your Corner of the World One Relationship At A Time." Part of what he shares is: "We are not destined to simply watch as our chaotic world slides into greater disorder. God's plan for changing the world involves each of us. You can change your corner of the world—one relationship at a time…The focus of Jesus' earthly ministry…embodies a passion for disciple-making that is generational and intentional…A disciple is a follower of Jesus: one who knows Him, tries to live as He lived, and never stops learning from Him; a lover of God and people…Disciple-making rarely happens by accident. It happens when one ordinary follower of Jesus intentionally invests in the lives of others…Discipling isn't always pretty. It doesn't always go according to plan. But there are people around you who would benefit from your efforts to help them learn to live and love like Jesus. You don't have to be a spiritual giant. Simply help them learn to walk with God, to live as Jesus lived, and to help others to follow Jesus! Anyone can engage in intentional, generational disciple-making. You just need to be a person who is willing to trust God to change the world, a few people at a time!"

The pastor-apologist must make certain that in his preparation and presentation he is careful and guarded against there being any missing ingredients. Eternity and the souls of people are important and requires one's best effort. The pastor-apologist should not think of his task as a mercenary who is focused on what his personal gain or status will be. Acceptable ministry is never about "me" but it must always be about Jesus only. As Paul approached and anticipated ministry, he indicated in Romans 1:14-17, "I am debtor both to Greeks and to Barbarians, both to the wise and to the foolish. So, as much as in me is, I am ready to preach the gospel to you also that are in Rome. For I am not ashamed of the gospel: for it is the power of God unto salvation to every one that believes; to the Jew first, and also to the Greek. For therein is revealed a righteousness of God from faith unto faith: as it is written, But the righteous shall live by faith." The commitment of Paul was: (1) I am a debtor (one who is obligated) to go, (2) I am ready (one who is eager) to preach the Gospel, and (3) I am not ashamed of the Gospel, it is the power of God unto salvation to everyone who believes.

If we are to prevent people from following the trend toward cultural captivity, we must make certain that there are no missing ingredients as we communicate God's Word to them. May God grant each of us a full measure of His wisdom and insight so that we will always handle the Word of God correctly and make it known with clarity.

17. Misfits and Other Idiosyncrasies

"The Misfits" was an American drama written by Arthur Miller. In 1961, it became a film that featured Clark Gable, Marilyn Monroe and Montgomery Clift. It became the final film appearance for Gable and Monroe. The storyline is about a beautiful recent divorcee who meets an aging cowboy. It is a typical story of lives that have experienced failure. They come together in the hope that they may find a basis for happiness. Small incidents that occur tend to prevent that from occurring. The meaning attached to Misfit is: "something that fits badly, as a garment that is too large or too small. or a person who is not suited or is unable to adjust to the circumstances of his or her particular situation." We can readily understand how easily the idea of idiosyncrasies can attach to misfits. The definition of idiosyncrasies is: "a characteristic, habit, mannerism, or the like, that is peculiar to an individual; the physical constitution peculiar to an individual." When these definitions are applied to religious choices or indifference, the concept and definition of misfits and idiosyncrasies begins to attach to those on a slippery slope that places those who are included within the trend toward cultural captivity.

As people are allowing for the Trend Toward Cultural Captivity in and for their lives, it appears they have made a choice for which there is no alternative left. They will become casualties of their own ill-advised choosing. They may appeal to victimization but that will only be valid as a consequence of the direction they sought. They are on the slippery slope and their momentum will only increase until they reach the point and place of no return. Slippery Slope had a particular meaning and application in Jeremiah 23. The term is frequently used in other areas where effort is made to diminish the reality of a slippery slope and the consequences for stepping onto it. On a National Public Radio Broadcast (July 2003), Fresh Air, Geoff Nunberg stated: "In the press, the phrase 'slippery slope' is more than seven times as common as it was twenty years ago. It's a convenient way of warning of the dire effects of some course of action without actually having to criticize the action itself..." In The Week (June 2013) James Graff indicated: "George Will once noted: All politics takes place on a slippery slope. That's never been more true, it seems, than now. Allowing gay marriage puts us on the slippery slope to polygamy and bestiality, opponents say; gun registration would start us sliding into the unconstitutional morass of universal arms confiscation. An NSA whistle-blower, William Binney, said last week that the agency's surveillance activities put us on a slippery slope toward a totalitarian state...And this week we're hearing a similar argument that President Obama's decision to arm Syrian rebels, however meagerly, has all but doomed us to an Iraq-style debacle...These critics may be right to urge caution, but in their panicked vehemence, they've abandoned nuance and succumbed to summoning up worst- case scenarios. UCLA law professor Eugene Volokh points out that metaphors like the slippery slope often start by enriching our vision and end by clouding it. Decriminalizing marijuana doesn't have to turn the United States into a stoner nation, nor does sending M-16s to Syrian rebels inevitably mean boots on the ground in Damascus. But that's not to say we shouldn't watch our footing." This is how a secular world looks at the slippery slope.

The reality of misfits and idiosyncrasies has surfaced within the broader missional work of the church. Many years ago, when missions was being pioneered in China by Hudson Taylor, a concern was raised regarding "going native" in order to gain access and rapport with the Chinese. In a Biography of Hudson James Taylor, the following is recorded: "The arrival of the largest party of missionaries ever sent to China, as well as their intent to be dressed in native clothing, gave the foreign settlement in Shanghai much to talk about and some criticism began for the young China Inland Mission. The party donned Chinese clothing, notwithstanding, even the women missionaries, which was deemed semi-scandalous at the time. When other missionaries sought to preserve their British ways, Taylor was convinced that the Gospel would only take root in Chinese soil if missionaries were willing to affirm the culture of the people they were seeking to reach. He argued, from the example of the Apostle Paul, "Let us in everything not sinful become like the Chinese, that by all means we may save some." This took on the flavor of the missionaries being misfits in the culture and possessing idiosyncrasies that were not necessarily conducive to the ministry objectives. More recently, David B. Gardner has written an article in A Voice of the Alliance of Confessing Evangelicals on June 12, 2014 entitled: *The Heart of the Insider Movement Paradigm*. He adds these thoughts: "Extreme practices of the Insider Movement Paradigm (IMP), like those missionaries who publicly convert to Islam in order to reach those in the mosque, are rejected even by most IM advocates. But the concerns before the Church of Jesus Christ around the world are not merely fringe excesses in IMP, but its wide and prevalent center and what we might call its soft forms…As I have witnessed in Bangladesh, IMP applied inevitably produces Islamized Christianity. In other IM contexts, Jesus gets cloaked in Buddhism and to Hinduism. The religion is different, the syncretism the same. IMP does not produce biblical Christianity but an ungodly merger of truth and error. The offspring of such unholy unions will always be hideous, helpless and hopeless…The faithful Church worldwide must arise, boldly advance biblical faith, and forbid any winsome presentation of error to win the day. No matter how compelling it sounds, error remains unfaithful and unloving. The IMP debate must not get framed in some false dichotomy between sterile confessionalism and gospel charity, between fearful theological retrenchment and courageous gospel advance, or between binding the Holy Spirit and relishing his dynamic ministry. Such categorizations are not only unbiblical, but are wholly unfair, unhelpful, and unloving…Further, now is no time to seek a big tent compromise or to view this debate as simply two equally valid yet differing opinions about missions. The IMP in all its versions operates with theological commitments incompatible with those of the historic Christian faith… So how far will we go? When will we concern ourselves again with theological integrity in missions? Perhaps the Apostle Paul puts the questions best in II Corinthians 6:14-16, "For what partnership has righteousness with lawlessness? Or what fellowship has light with darkness? What accord has Christ with Belial? Or what portion does a believer share with an unbeliever? What agreement has the temple of God with idols?" The IMP does not present the gospel faithfully and is therefore not faithful missions. We must not pretend, for any reason, that it is. We must not become complicit theologically, missionally, or financially in any agreement of the temple of God with idols." Once again, lurking in the background is a national resistance to that which appears to impress others. Those who are indulging in such practices are misfits who may be driven solely by their personal idiosyncrasies.

When one scans the landscape of religious broadcasting, it becomes obvious wherein a festering problem exists. If one watched any one of the religious television networks, all kinds of divergent views would be viewed and confusion would become a factor. There are misfits with their idiosyncrasies broadcasting their beliefs and propaganda every day. There appears to be no limit to their creativity and misrepresentations. Some take on a theatrical appearance, whereas others present a format of informative study. It tries to identify itself as being largely and broadly evangelical. However, in the ebb and flow of cultural practices and the attempt of the church to adapt and appeal to it, compromises are being made and the message of Scripture is being diminished. It becomes a distraction that drives people away. Because of these distractions, how close is the world, nation, culture and society to the precipitous slippery slope?

If there was a will and desire to listen and heed a word from the Lord, they might hear these words from Jeremiah 23:9-14 (MSG) for our day and time. The Prophet writes: "My head is reeling, my limbs are limp, I'm staggering like a drunk, seeing double from too much wine. and all because of God, because of his holy words. Now for what God says regarding the lying prophets: Can you believe it? A country teeming with adulterers - faithless, promiscuous idolater-adulterers! They're a curse on the land. The land is a wasteland. Their unfaithfulness is turning the country into a cesspool, Prophets and priests devoted to desecration. They have nothing to do with me as their God. My very own Temple, mind you is mud-spattered with their crimes. But they won't get by with it. They'll find themselves on a slippery slope, careening into the darkness, somersaulting into the pitch-black dark. I'll make them pay for their crimes. It will be the Year of Doom. Over in Samaria I saw prophets acting like silly fools. Shocking! They preached using that no-god Baal for a text, messing with the minds of my people. And the Jerusalem prophets are even worse. Horrible, sex-driven, living a lie, subsidizing a culture of wickedness, and never giving it a second thought. They're as bad as those wretches in old Sodom, the degenerates of old Gomorrah."

The Scriptures are clear regarding the abominable behavior and practices of those who lived in Sodom and Gomorrah. In God's sight, it matters little how the church of today attempts to redefine that which God has explicitly declared. The cultural-oriented church of this day is trying to appeal to the trends by presenting a message that condones that which God long ago had condemned. The references to Sodom and Gomorrah in Scripture always have a negative and condemnatory tone. Despite all the redefinition of terms, God cannot be redefined and reshaped to be made acceptable to those who have become willing cultural captives. Some of the Scriptures that address the wickedness of the inhabitants of Sodom and Gomorrah are: Genesis 13:13, 19:4-13; Deuteronomy 32:32; Isaiah 3:9; Jeremiah 23:14; Lamentations 4:6; Ezekiel 16:46-49 and Jude 1:7. The Scriptures that speak of the destruction of Sodom and Gomorrah on account of the wickedness of the people are: Genesis 19:1-29; Deuteronomy 29:23; Isaiah 13:19; Jeremiah 49:18 and 50:40; Lamentations 4:6; Amos 4:11; Zephaniah 2:9; Matthew 10:15; Luke 17:29; Romans 9:29 and II Peter 2:6.

From the above lists, Lamentations 4:6 states: "For the iniquity of the daughter of my people is greater than the sin of Sodom, that was overthrown as in a moment…" In Ezekiel 16:48-49, we read: "As I live, saith the Lord Jehovah, Sodom thy sister hath not done, she nor her daughters, as thou hast done, thou and thy daughters. Behold, this was the iniquity of thy sister Sodom:

pride, fullness of bread, and prosperous ease was in her and in her daughters; neither did she strengthen the hand of the poor and needy." Zephaniah 2:9 indicates: "Therefore as I live, saith Jehovah of hosts, the God of Israel, surely Moab shall be as Sodom, and the children of Ammon as Gomorrah, a possession of nettles, and salt pits, and a perpetual desolation: the residue of my people shall make a prey of them, and the remnant of my nation shall inherit them." Romans 9:29 states: "And, as Isaiah hath said before: Except the Lord of the Sabbath had left us a seed, we had become as Sodom, and had been made like unto Gomorrah." These and other verses speak of the standard of God as the dictate for acceptable and righteous behavior. The influences of the LGBT and the readiness of the modern organization that calls itself the church to be complicit will only increase, enhance and accelerate the trend toward cultural captivity.

18. Detriments and Impediments

This chapter will consider some of the detriments and impediments to righteousness. The place where we begin is to determine: What is righteousness? In terms of a Biblical follower of Christ, it is "the state of moral perfection required by God to enter heaven." The secular definition is: "one who is strictly observant of morality: always behaving according to a religious or moral code; that which is justifiable: considered to be correct or justifiable; one who is responding to injustice: arising from the perception of great injustice or wrongdoing." When we think of the choices being made in and by the culture of this day, whether we use the spiritual definition or the secular, is the overall trend toward righteousness? A reason for asking this question and analyzing where we are today is based on Proverbs 14:34, "Righteousness exalts a nation; but sin is a reproach to any people." On this basis, a question that should be asked and answered is: Are we a nation and culture that is marked by righteousness? Are we a culture that is in the category of being exalted? Are we a nation deserving of condemnation and judgment?

The defining moment for any person or culture is the decision and choice one makes about Jesus Christ. He stands at the crossroad for everyone in every generation. It is not a ground of neutrality. A decision and choice must be made at that moment of time. Why is Jesus Christ central to whether or not a person or culture is embracing righteousness? The answer is because righteousness and Jesus Christ are synonymous. If one has Jesus Christ, he/she also has righteousness. If one wants true righteousness, one must truly want Jesus Christ. The response is based upon II Corinthians 5:21 (ESV), "For our sake he made him to be sin who knew no sin, so that in him we might become the righteousness of God." The NLT states the verse: "For God made Christ, who never sinned, to be the offering for our sin, so that we could be made right with God through Christ." Jesus Christ is the one and only source for righteousness in one's life and within one's culture. Paul summarized his desire and pursuit for righteousness in Philippians 3:9, "I want to…be found in him, not having a righteousness of my own that comes from the law, but that which comes through faith in Christ, the righteousness from God that depends on faith." There is a hymn where the refrain asks: "What will you do with Jesus, neutral you cannot be? Someday your heart will be asking, what will He do with me?"

The larger question is: What are we doing with Jesus? Why are there glaring areas of detriment and impediment? Why is the church that is supposed to be representing the message of Jesus Christ to our generation and culture diminishing in numbers, influence and impact? Why is it that the Bible and prayer in Jesus name has become an object for scorn and repudiation? Why is it that righteousness is waning in our nation, culture and world? Is the church itself at the crossroad in terms of Jesus Christ and His message or is it in His crosshairs for having squandered its opportunities and ignored its mission? Have we as individuals been good soldiers of Jesus Christ or have we gone AWOL (Absent With Out Leave)?

One possible detriment and impediment in terms of righteousness and the influence of the church in today's culture may have something to do with the virtue, integrity and character of those have been chosen to be a pastor in and for a congregation. If "The Thriving Pastor" (from Focus On The Family) for June 9th, 2014 is correct, there is a growing detriment and impediment in and for the church today. The following was taken from: 4 PERIMETERS TO PROTECT YOUR MARRIAGE by Jesse Rincones. He begins his column with some poignant observations from the following headlines: (1) "Mega- church Pastor Shocks Congregation With Abrupt Resignation After Confessing to a Moral Failing." (2) "Pastor Resigns After Admitting Infidelity." And (3) "Pastor Steps Down After Cheating On His Wife." He added a frightening statistic: "Some say 1 in 2.7 men will cheat on their wives. Others say 60% of men and 40% of women will have an affair. Other numbers hit closer to home: 30% of male Protestant ministers have had sexual relationships with women other than their wives. One area not discussed in the article is pornography. Many Pastors have to deal with the temptation of pornography in their personal lives and marriages. It is one of the more subtle and diabolical temptations that is available via the Internet as well as other sources. The numbers regarding failed marriages may vary, but the risk is clear." Another subtle area is plagiarism and how someone else's sermon preparation or study is taken and represented as being one's own work product. This failure in personal lives of ministers and religious leaders impacts moral values and influence within the culture. It is more of a victory chant of the culture than it is a testimonial about the church and its purpose for existing.

In a recent Breakpoint: Pastor To Pastor by T. M. Moore, reference is made to the important discipline of personal self-watch. Attention is drawn to the important application of a passage such as I Timothy 4:12-16, "Let no man despise thy youth; but be thou an example to them that believe, in word, in manner of life, in love, in faith, in purity. Till I come, give heed to reading, to exhortation, to teaching. Neglect not the gift that is in thee, which was given thee by prophecy, with the laying on of the hands of the presbytery. Be diligent in these things; give thyself wholly to them; that thy progress may be manifest unto all. Take heed to thyself, and to thy teaching. Continue in these things; for in doing this thou shalt save both thyself and them that hear thee." T. M. Moore continues with this timely and vital reminder: "The man of virtue understands that the heart is deceitful and desperately wicked. That it too readily surrenders to the law of sin, giving passion free rein to lead us into anger, lust, resentment, vindictiveness, and other dangerous affections."

There is great wisdom and need for one to allot much time in the Word of God and for prayer application being made with words such as Psalm 139:23-24, "Search me, O God, and know my heart: Try me, and know my thoughts; and see if there be any wicked way in me, and lead me in the way everlasting." In a similar way, the words of Psalm 19:12-14 should be verbalized before the

Lord in prayer: "Who can discern his errors? Clear thou me from hidden faults. Keep back thy servant also from presumptuous sins; let them not have dominion over me: then shall I be upright, and I shall be clear from great transgression. Let the words of my mouth and the meditation of my heart be acceptable in thy sight, O Jehovah, my Lord, my rock, and my redeemer." There is also the needed reminder of the words shared by Paul in Ephesians 5:15-17, "Look therefore carefully how you walk, not as unwise, but as wise; redeeming the time, because the days are evil. Wherefore do not be foolish, but understand what the will of the Lord is." If one is desirous of being a person of virtue, there must be nourishment of the soul with that which contributes to one's purity and virtue.

The remainder of the Thriving Pastor article has a focus on "Perimeter Protection." Reference is made to the Handbook for the United States Department of the Interior as it discusses the protection of its facilities. It states: "Perimeter protection is the first line of defense in providing physical security for a facility." The Thriving Pastor application is: "The principle of using perimeter protection to protect our nation's facilities is also one that can prove invaluable to the protection of your marriage." According to the government handbook on perimeters, "Every vulnerable point should be protected to deter or prevent unauthorized access." The first vulnerable point that must be protected within a perimeter is the eyes. Their concern: Visual Alertness and Discipline. The emphasis is: "Don't Become Distracted By Looking At Wrong Things."

A Sunday School Teacher faithfully reminded his class of boys to memorize and do Psalm 1 throughout their lives. Over the years, Psalm 1:1-2 (NKJV) comes often to mind: "Blessed is the man who walks not in the counsel of the ungodly, nor stands in the path of sinners, nor sits in the seat of the scornful; but his delight is in the law of the Lord, and in His law he meditates day and night." As the Sunday School Teacher had taught us: The progression of innocuous sin becomes obvious: The first step is the walking in the pathway of sinners. The second step is standing in the pathway of sinners (suggesting a longing for and gazing at that which is inappropriate). The third step is sitting in the seat of the scorners (being comfortable in an association and camaraderie with those who have an apathy or denial toward spiritual truths).

As The Thriving Pastor article states: "Once the eyes have allowed a perimeter violation, it's not long before greater curiosity kicks in. A violation of the visual perimeter will require the enforcement of the mental and emotional perimeter." A invaluable personal guideline was also shared by the faithful Sunday School Teacher with his class of boys. It was taken from Proverbs 4:20-27 where Solomon wrote: "My son, be attentive to my words; incline your ear to my sayings. Let them not escape from your sight; keep them within your heart. For they are life to those who find them, and healing to all their flesh." What were the necessary principles and guidelines that Solomon was promulgating for one's life? They are: (1) Keep your heart with all vigilance (and diligence), for from it flow the springs (issues) of life. (2) Put away from you crooked speech, and (3) put devious talk far from you. (4) Let your eyes look directly forward, and your gaze be straight before you. (5) Ponder the path of your feet; then all your ways will be sure. (6) Do not swerve to the right or to the left; (7) turn your foot away from evil.

How does a pastor lose his focus? What is it that causes him to sacrifice his virtue and integrity? Has he allowed for a false presumption about vulnerability and the power of temptation? Has he allowed for temptation to be short-circuited in his thinking so that he ignores the danger and peril that is attached to it? Has he failed to remind himself of James 1:13-15? "Let no man say when he is tempted, I am tempted of God; for God cannot be tempted with evil, and he himself tempts no man: but each man is tempted, when he is drawn away by his own lust, and enticed. Then the lust, when it hath conceived, bears sin: and the sin, when it is full grown, brings forth death."

In practical areas for one's life, there needs to be a reminder of at least three dangers: (1) There can be a wrong focus, Psalm 73:2-3, "But as for me, my feet were almost gone; my steps had well nigh slipped. For I was envious at the foolish, when I saw the prosperity of the wicked." Is it possible that one can too easily and readily allow digression from a narrow visual perimeter and focus? This would be a case of losing sight of the goal and finish line and looking at other things in other places. (2) There can be a wrong pathway, Psalm 94:17-21, "Unless the Lord had been my help, my soul had almost dwelt in silence. When I said: My foot slips; Thy mercy, O Lord, held me up." We need to implement the words of Psalm 23, "The Lord is my Shepherd…He leads me in the paths of righteousness for His name's sake…goodness and mercy will follow me all the days of my life." This should be the place of our commitment and contentment. (3) There can be a wrong attitude, Hebrews 2:1-4. "Therefore we ought to give the more earnest heed to the things which we have heard, lest at any time we should let them slip. For if the word spoken by angels was steadfast, and every transgression and disobedience received a just recompense of reward; How shall we escape, if we neglect so great salvation; which at the first began to be spoken by the Lord, and was confirmed unto us by them that heard him; God also bearing them witness, both with signs and wonders, and with divers miracles, and gifts of the Holy Ghost, according to his own will…" We should never digress from the teaching and principles of God's Word. We should never ignore or reinterpret it. There are far too many detriments and impediments to righteousness in the culture whose trend is toward cultural captivity.

How should you be living during uncertain times? How assertive should you and the church be in the current culture and trends? What should your personal role and commitment be in a day where many have rejected the Lord? What will your personal role be? Will you be a spectator or a participator in terms of the task to be done? Will you be a good and faithful soldier of the Lord Jesus Christ or will you be AWOL? The Gospel of the Lord Jesus Christ is clear and plain, I John 5:12-13, "He that hath the Son hath the life; he that hath not the Son of God hath not the life. These things have I written unto you, that you may know that ye have eternal life, even unto you that believe on the name of the Son of God." Do you believe this Gospel? If so, then you should both live it and proclaim it! May the Lord grant you the courage and boldness to do that for Him. We have a generation whose trend is toward cultural captivity. We need to do our part to warn them of the awaiting peril. We should also endeavor to convince them to reverse their course and escape the consequences of cultural captivity.

19. Incalculable Imputations

The subject of imputation is both broad and all-encompassing. If one is to understand the current trend toward cultural captivity, there must be an understanding about original sin and how it has been passed down to all generations. CARM (Christian Apologetics and Research Ministry) offers the following as a workable definition of original sin. Their statement is: "Original sin is known in two senses: (1) the Fall of Adam as the original sin and (2) the hereditary fallen nature and moral corruption that is passed down from Adam to his descendants. It is called original in that Adam, the first man, is the one who sinned and thus caused sin to enter the world…Original sin is not a physical corruption but a moral and spiritual corruption. It could be compared to the Reformed Doctrine of Total Depravity which states that sin has touched all parts of what a person is: heart, mind, soul, will, thoughts and desires."

There are at least two significant passages in this regard. First, I Timothy 2:11-15 states: "Let a woman learn in quietness with all subjection. But I permit not a woman to teach, nor to have dominion over a man, but to be in quietness. For Adam was first formed, then Eve; and Adam was not beguiled, but the woman being beguiled hath fallen into transgression: but she shall be saved through her child- bearing, if they continue in faith and love and sanctification with sobriety." Verse 14 should be noted: "Adam was not beguiled, but the woman having been beguiled has fallen into transgression." In the strictest sense of the logical order of events, the serpent approached Eve first and gave her his rationale to which she became convinced and quickly succumbed. At this point, Eve had disobeyed God and had brought about the disrupted fellowship with Him. What about Adam? He wasn't there during the dialogue between the serpent and Eve. In actuality, he had not yet succumbed to any temptation or act of disobedience. When Eve approached Adam, and he allowed himself to do what he knew was wrong, he voluntarily entered into the act of disobedience and both of them were now alienated from God. At that point, they connived together how they might hide themselves and their act of disobedience from their Creator. They thought if they found a place of refuge and obscurity they would escape the scrutiny of God. It was at this point that The Trend Toward Cultural Captivity began.

The second significant passage is Romans 5:12-21. It is a description of what this act of disobedience meant and engendered for humanity from that point forward. It addresses the scope of the offense and the provision of grace. The concept of imputation is shared in terms of both the trespass that had been committed as well as the act of grace that was providing resolve to the dilemma of the human race. The words written by Paul are: "Therefore, as through one man sin entered into the world, and death through sin; and so death passed unto all men, for that all sinned. For until the law sin was in the world, but sin is not imputed when there is no law. Nevertheless death reigned from Adam until Moses, even over them that had not sinned after the likeness of Adam's transgression...For if by the trespass of the one the many died, much more did the grace of God, and the gift by the grace of the one man, Jesus Christ, abound unto the many. And not as through one that sinned, so is the gift: for the judgment came of one unto condemnation, but the free gift came of many trespasses unto justification. For if, by the trespass of the one, death reigned through the one; much more shall they that receive the abundance of grace and of the gift of righteousness reign in life through the one, even Jesus Christ. So then as through one trespass the judgment came unto all men to condemnation; even so through one act of righteousness the free gift came unto all men to justification of life. For as through the one man's disobedience the many were made sinners, even so through the obedience of the one shall the many be made righteous. And the law came in besides, that the trespass might abound; but where sin abounded, grace did abound more exceedingly: that, as sin reigned in death, even so might grace reign through righteousness unto eternal life through Jesus Christ our Lord."

The terms used in these verses have special meaning. Easton's Bible Dictionary states: Imputation means: "to designate any action, word or thing as reckoned to a person. Thus in doctrinal language (1) the sin of Adam is imputed to all his descendants, i.e., it is reckoned as theirs, and they are dealt with therefore as guilty; (2) the righteousness of Christ is imputed to them that believe in him, or so attributed to them as to be considered their own; and (3) our sins are imputed to Christ, i.e., He assumed our law-place, undertook to answer the demands of justice for our sins. In all these cases the nature of imputation is the same (Romans 5:12-19; and Philemon 1:18, 19). The idea of Divine Justice being satisfied and Imputation of Righteousness now being made available is referenced in Isaiah 53:10-11 (ESV): "Yet it was the will of the Lord to crush him; He has put him to grief; when his soul makes an offering for guilt, He shall see His offspring; He shall prolong his days; the will of the Lord shall prosper in his hand. Out of the anguish of His soul he shall see and be satisfied; by his knowledge shall the righteous one, my servant, make many to be accounted righteous, and he shall bear their iniquities." What a great and gracious act and provision from a just and loving God!

A special illustration of this provision of a gracious and just God is Paul's letter to Philemon. It is a unique letter in that Paul has been making an appeal in behalf of one of Philemon's runaway slaves, Onesimus. Paul has met with this slave and he has become a follower of Christ. Paul has informed Onesimus that he must return to Philemon. Paul makes an appeal to Philemon to be kind and gracious to this slave. The passage states (ESV): "If he has wronged you at all, or owes you anything, charge that to my account. I, Paul, write this with my own hand: I will repay it, to say nothing of you owing me even your own self." Paul is willing for any debt of Onesimus to be imputed to him and he will accept the obligation to make full payment or restitution for that which is owed. The words of Paul are very compelling. In verses 8-12 (NLT), Paul writes a very personal request to Philemon, "I am boldly asking a favor of you. I could demand it in the name of Christ because it is the right thing for you to do, but because of our love, I prefer just to ask you.

So take this as a request from your friend Paul, an old man, now in prison for the sake of Christ Jesus. My plea is that you show kindness to Onesimus. I think of him as my own son because he became a believer as a result of my ministry here in prison. Onesimus hasn't been of much use to you in the past, but now he is very useful to both of us. I am sending him back to you, and with him comes my own heart." It is an appeal for compassion, kindness, forgiveness, acceptance and restoration. In the culture of slavery, it is not the way a slave-holder would usually respond to a runaway slave. One can also easily wonder if Philemon will make a connection between his actual runaway slave and the way Paul referred to himself in most of the epistles he wrote and sent. The opening words would be: "Paul, a bond-servant (or slave) of Jesus Christ." Paul concludes his letter to Philemon with an additional word of encouragement and expectation in Verses 21-22 (NLT), "I am confident as I write this letter that you will do what I ask and even more! Please keep a guest room ready for me, for I am hoping that God will answer your prayers and let me return to you soon."

Easton's Dictionary goes on to discuss "The Threefold Use of the Term (Imputation) in Theology: Original Sin, Atonement and Justification." Easton writes: "Three acts of imputation are given special prominence in the Scripture, and are implicated in the Scriptural doctrines of Original Sin, Atonement and Justification...the term imputation has been used in theology in a threefold sense to denote the judicial acts of God by which the guilt of Adam's sin is imputed to his posterity; by which the sins of Christ's people are imputed to Him; and by which the righteousness of Christ is imputed to His people. The act of imputation is precisely the same in each case. It is not meant that Adam's sin was personally the sin of his descendants, but that it was set to their account, so that they share its guilt and penalty. It is not meant that Christ shares personally in the sins of men, but that the guilt of his people's sin was set to his account, so that He bore its penalty. It is not meant that Christ's people are made personally holy or inwardly righteous by the imputation of His righteousness to them, but that

His righteousness is set to their account, so that they are entitled to all the rewards of that perfect righteousness. These doctrines have had a place in theology of the Christian church from the earliest Christian centuries, though the doctrine of the imputation of the righteousness of Christ was first fully and clearly stated at the time of and following the Reformation. The first two of these doctrines have been the possession of the entire Christian church, while the third one of them is affirmed by both the Reformed and Lutheran branches of Protestantism."

W. H. Griffith-Thomas, a Biblical scholar of the late 19th and early 20th century, shared some thoughts from the Book of Hebrews under a general heading: The Danger of Drifting (Hebrews 1:1–2:4), "Incorporated within the very framework and message of the book of Hebrews are five danger signals. These are like stop signs on the boulevard of backsliding. They are warning posters placed on the freeway of disobedience: (1) Chapter 2, The danger of drifting; (2) Chapters 3-4, The danger of not entering into rest; (3) Chapters 5-6, The danger of not going on to maturity; (4) Chapter 10, The danger of willful sin; and (5) Chapter 12, The danger of indifference to the point of denial. There is a progression in these warnings. It starts with being careless about salvation and indifferent to spiritual things until finally one comes to be perfectly satisfied with being indifferent. He has also has stated for these five warnings: (1) Don't Drift - Drifting (2:1-4); (2) Don't Doubt - Doubting (3:7–4:13); (3) Don't Degenerate - Deformity (5:11–6:20); (4) Don't Despise - Despising (10:26-31) and (5) Don't Depart - Denying (12:15-29)." If one would read and heed these warnings, it would be instructive so one can avoid the pathway and Trend Toward Cultural Captivity.

What if one has ignored the warnings and instructions listed above and erred by stepping across the threshold onto the slippery slope, is there any possibility of reclamation and restoration for such a one? There are words of hope and potential for anyone with sense enough to seek the Lord without any further delay. The words in Joel 2:12-13 are encouraging and helpful. These words are from the Lord to a people who had been devastated because of their rebellion and sin: "Yet even now, saith Jehovah, turn unto me with all your heart, and with fasting, and with weeping, and with mourning: and rend your heart, and not your garments, and turn unto Jehovah your God; for he is gracious and merciful, slow to anger, and abundant in lovingkindness…" In Joel 2:25-27 are additional words of hope and promise: "And I will restore to you the years that the locust hath eaten, the canker-worm, and the caterpillar, and the palmer-worm, my great army which I sent among you. And you shall eat in plenty and be satisfied, and shall praise the name of Jehovah your God, that hath dealt wondrously with you; and my people shall never be put to shame. And you shall know that I am in the midst of Israel, and that I am Jehovah your God, and there is none else; and my people shall never be put to shame." In Joel 2:28-32 (selected) are the words indicating God's intention to bless His people in unique ways: "And it shall come to pass afterward, that I will pour out my Spirit upon all flesh; and your sons and your daughters shall prophesy, your old men shall dream dreams, your young men shall see visions: and also upon the servants and upon the handmaids in those days will I pour out my Spirit…And it shall come to pass, that whosoever shall call on the name of Jehovah shall be delivered; for in mount Zion and in Jerusalem there shall be those that escape, as Jehovah hath said, and among the remnant those whom Jehovah doth call." Interestingly, this passage is referenced by Peter in Acts 2:15-22 as the Day of Pentecost has dawned and God's power and plan is being evidenced. As one responds to the Lord and His message, it will free him/her from the Trend Toward Cultural Captivity and set one on a pathway of deliverance and blessing. Have you responded to the Lord? Are you walking in His ways day by day?

20. Escape From Cultural Captivity

On July 4, 2014, A Fox Online News Summary Page had this Headline Section: " Real Freedom Took Real Courage" by Chris Stirewalt. While his comments are on the subject of politics and politicians, it is easy enough to make a transition into the realm of religion. His political comments included: "Political courage these days is generally defined as a politician doing something that might make it harder to get re-elected. Real civic leadership has always been about convincing people to do what's right and hard rather than what's popular and easy. Courage is part of that. People are less likely to follow a leader who asks them to sacrifice and struggle when he or she will not. But now, that sacrifice generally refers to a politician having to spend more of other peoples' money on a primary election contest or, in rare cases, moving to a lucrative career in punditry or influence peddling sooner than expected. The courage of defying voters to give lobbyists and press hounds what they want in exchange for a lobbying job or to join the press pack is not exactly shivering with the troops at Valley Forge. In fact it's not really courage at all. On Independence Day, Americans do not celebrate actual independence from Britain, which didn't formally come until the signing of the Treaty of Paris on September 3, 1783. Nor do we celebrate the start of the revolution that would make us free, which began in Massachusetts on April 19, 1775 and lasted for eight years. What we celebrate is the act of declaring our independence; the ratification and signing of a document that was meaningless without the might of arms to make it so. What we celebrate are the ideas in the Declaration of Independence, that most remarkable piece of political writing in history, and the courage of the politicians who engaged in what was seen by the duly established authorities as treason."

Theodore Roosevelt, the twenty-sixth President of the United States made these comments in various speeches: "To educate a person in the mind but not in morals is to educate a menace to society...Knowing what's right doesn't mean much unless you do what's right...In any moment of decision, the best thing you can do is the right thing. The worst thing you can do is nothing...No one cares how much you know, until they know how much you care." This is clearly a Biblical principle that should be part of the fabric of one's being. James 4:17 (NKJV), James was both terse and clear when he wrote: "to him who knows to do good and does not do it, to him it is sin." This is similar to the clear and precise statement in I John 3:4-10 (NKJV), "Whoever commits sin also commits lawlessness, and sin is lawlessness. And you know that He was manifested to take away our sins, and in Him there is no sin. Whoever abides in Him does not sin. Whoever sins has neither seen Him nor known Him. Little children, let no one deceive you. He who practices righteousness is righteous, just as He is righteous. He who sins is of the devil, for the devil has sinned from the beginning. For this purpose the Son of God was manifested, that He might destroy the works of the devil. Whoever has been born of God does not sin, for His seed remains in him; and he cannot sin, because he has been born of God. In this the children of God and the children of the devil are manifest: Whoever does not practice righteousness is not of God, nor is he who does not love his brother."

John is not teaching sinless perfection. He is teaching that the one who has confessed Jesus Christ as Savior and Lord will be one who sins less. It is the process of old things passing away and all things becoming new. Justification is an ACT of God's free grace whereas Sanctification is a WORK of God's free grace. This translates over to that which a person practices. If Christ is making the difference in one's life, then righteousness will be one's quality of life and modeled characteristic. If one's life continues down a pathway of blatant sin and disobedience, that one may make a profession but the reality of it is challenged by the behavior and practice of that life and lifestyle. The focus and commitment of one's life in Christ should be the areas of growth, development and completeness in Christ.

It is alleged that William Carey, who pioneered missionary endeavor in India, wrote to his sons on his seventieth birthday.

Some of his words were: "I am this day seventy years old, a monument of Divine mercy and goodness, though on a review of my life I find much, very much, for which I ought to be humbled in the dust, my direct and positive sins are innumerable, my negligence in the Lord's work has been great, I have not promoted his cause, nor sought his glory and honor as I ought, not withstanding all this, I am spared till now, and am still retained in His Work, and I trust I am received into the divine favor through him." How would you review your life and accomplishments in terms of God and His will for your life? Are you following a "well done, good and faithful servant" path, or are you following "depart from Me…I never knew you" path? Do you share a William Carey hope and expectation? What is your personal basis for that hope and expectation?

Some thought should be given to the Word of God and how it should be impacting one's life and active behavior. Cautionary and instructive words are stated in passages such as Colossians 2:8-10 (ASV), "Take heed lest there shall be anyone that makes spoil of you through his philosophy and vain deceit, after the tradition of men, after the rudiments of the world, and not after Christ: for in him dwells all the fullness of the Godhead bodily, and in him ye are made full, who is the head of all principality and power…" To the church at Philippi, Paul encouraged them to remember the words in Philippians 1:6, "being confident of this very thing, that he who began a good work in you will perfect it until the day of Jesus Christ…" In this process of becoming complete in Jesus Christ, Paul reminded the believers in Philippians 2:13-15, "So then, my beloved, even as ye have always obeyed, not as in my presence only, but now much more in my absence, work out your own salvation with fear and trembling; for it is God who works in you both to will and to work, for his good pleasure. Do all things without murmurings and questionings: that ye may become blameless and harmless, children of God without blemish in the midst of a crooked and perverse generation, among whom ye are seen as lights in the world."

All of this has significance when he emphasizes that they are to be: "children of God without blemish in the midst of a crooked and perverse generation, among whom you are seen as lights in the world." The crooked and perverse generation would like to force as many as possible into its mold. If one succumbs and follows in that pathway, it will be the Trend Toward Cultural Captivity and, more than likely, ultimate eternal death. Paul holds out the standard for the follower of Christ in the words "that you may become blameless and harmless, children of God without blemish." This is the path of personal victory that will allow one to escape all the lure of cultural captivity. J. B. Philipps gives the force of Colossians 2:9-10 when he translates: "Yet it is in him that God gives a full and complete expression of himself (within the physical limits that he set himself in Christ). Moreover, your own completeness is only realized in him, who is the authority over all authorities, and the supreme power over all powers." Note the idea and beauty of what is being expressed: "God gives a full and complete expression of himself" and that is the certainty of every follower of Jesus Christ. J. B. Philipps makes it clear that: "Your own completeness is only realized in him." You are complete only in Him.

In a day and time of cultural chaos and captivity, the prophet of God spoke a message of judgment to a scattered and disinterested generation. At the moment of considerable distress, Jeremiah cries out to God. In Jeremiah 10:23-24 (NIV), as he pours out his heart before God, he prays: "I know, O Lord, that the way of man is not in himself, that it is not in man who walks to direct his steps. Correct me, O Lord, but in justice; not in your anger, lest you bring me to nothing." The context is in verses 21-22, 25: "The shepherds are senseless and do not inquire of the Lord; so they do not prosper and all their flock is scattered. Listen! The report is coming - a great commotion from the land of the North! It will make the towns of Judah desolate, a haunt of jackals...Pour out your wrath on the nations that do not acknowledge you, on the peoples who do not call on your name. For they have devoured Jacob; they have devoured him completely and destroyed his homeland." It describes the dreadful day of sin and captivity. In the bleakness and distress, Jeremiah knows and shares the right path for deliverance and escape. If only they would hear and heed the heart cry of the prophet of God, but they continue in their pernicious (ruinous, hurtful, injurious, fatal) ways with little or no regard for the immediacy of the disaster that awaits them as they head toward the slippery slope. What message do you think the prophet would be sharing with our nation? Do we have any sense of the gravity of the times in which we are living? Are we a nation that is honoring God in our schools, churches and government? What do you believe it will take to get the attention of people in this nation to once again seek and exalt the Lord?

This obstinate refusal to turn from their pathway reminds one of the question asked in Hebrews 2:1-3 (NIV), "We must pay more careful attention…to what we have heard, so that we do not drift away. For if the message spoken by angels was binding, and every violation and disobedience received its just punishment, how shall we escape if we ignore such a great salvation? This salvation, which was first announced by the Lord, was confirmed to us by those who heard him…" The MSG paraphrase of this passage is: "It's crucial that we keep a firm grip on what we've heard so that we don't drift off. If the old message delivered by the angels was valid and nobody got away with anything, do you think we can risk neglecting this latest message, this magnificent salvation? First of all, it was delivered in person by the Master, then accurately passed on to us by those who heard it from him…" A portion of this paraphrase that will haunt many throughout eternity is: "Do you think we can risk neglecting this latest message, this magnificent salvation?" They will know, regrettably much too late, their neglect resulted in their own loss and eternal condemnation.

In a sermon preached by Charles H. Spurgeon on the subject of Complete In Him, some of his thoughts were: "COMPLETE IN HIM! Oh! may we by grace be made to see that they really are ours, for ours they are if we answer to the character described in the opening verses of the Epistle to the Colossians. If we have faith in Jesus Christ, love towards all the saints, and a hope laid up in heaven, we may grasp this golden sentence as all our own…Have you been able to follow in that which has already been described as the way which leads from banishment? Then you may take this choice sentence to yourself as a portion of your inheritance; for weak, poor, helpless, unworthy though you are in yourself, IN HIM, your Lord, your Redeemer, you are complete in the fullest, broadest, and most varied sense of that mighty word, and you will be glad to muse upon the wonders of this glorious position." This is you place of completeness, refuge and assurance if you grasp it by faith.

Spurgeon's sermon continued with these thoughts about the meaning and implication of what being complete in Him truly means. He said: "(1) You are Complete in Him without the aid of Jewish Ceremonies; (2) You are complete in Him without the help of Philosophy; (3) You are complete in Him without the inventions of Superstition; and (4) You are complete in Him without Human Merit (our own works being regarded as filthy rags)." He adds a summary comment: "Rejoice, then, that you are complete in Him.' Look on your own nothingness and be humble, but look at Jesus, your great Representative, and be glad. Be not so intent upon your own corruptions as to forget His immaculate purity, which He has given to you. Be not so mindful of your original poverty as to forget the infinite riches which He has conferred on you. It will save you many pangs if you will learn to think of yourself as being IN HIM, and as being by His glorious grace accepted in Him, and perfect in Christ Jesus." This can be your assurance, completeness and victory in the Lord Jesus Christ. Are you complete in Him? Do you know His glorious grace and the assurance of being accepted in Him?

One of the great Hymns that surfaced in the twentieth century was: *How Great Thou Art*. It was written by Carl Boberg (1859-1940), English Translation by Stuart K. Hine (1899-1989), and popularized by George Beverly Shea during the New York City Billy Graham Crusade in 1957. The fourth stanza contains the resounding expectation for all those whose hope and confidence is in Jesus Christ for their completeness and victory. The words are: "When Christ shall come, with shouts of acclamation, and take me home, what joy shall fill my heart! Then I shall bow in humble adoration and there proclaim, My God, how great Thou art!" This is the ultimate and final deliverance from any and every Trend Toward

Cultural Captivity. Have you received this deliverance in Jesus Christ?

Final Word

Events in the world are changing very rapidly. The United States has chosen to step back from the exceptional role where it was recognized as being the Number One Country in the world. When that was done, it created a vacuum. Terrorist organizations and other world powers no longer saw any nation that would offer resistance to their aims and ambitions. As this book was being written, we saw Russia seize Crimea and set designs for other portions of Ukraine. The Islamic State took over portions of Syria and Iraq. They seized key cities in Iraq and military equipment. In the process, they operated on the basis of Sharia Law and are not hesitant to kill anyone who will not be loyal to the movement. Christians were ordered to convert to Islam or to leave their homes and cities. When they failed to comply, they were given a deadline to leave and it required they do so without taking any of their possessions. In addition to the various Middle Eastern tensions, Israel and Hamas (in Gaza) have been engaged in armed conflict. Multitudes of people, many of them children, from Guatemala, Honduras, El Salvador and Mexico have been taking advantage of the porous borders of the United States and have streamed across the Rio Grande and given refuge.

It would be easy for one to conclude that this is the beginning of the end. It may very well be a prelude of things to come. If it is, how should we be living? What should we be doing? In his day, the Psalmist considered a question recorded in Psalm 11:3 (ASV), "If the foundations be destroyed, What can the righteous do?" When Paul wrote to the Thessalonian believers about the nearness of the end times, he included these words in I Thessalonians 5:1-6 (ASV), "But concerning the times and the seasons...you have no need that anything be written unto you. For yourselves know perfectly that the day of the Lord so comes as a thief in the night. When they are saying, Peace and safety, then sudden destruction comes upon them, as travail upon a woman with child; and they shall in no wise escape. But you…are not in darkness, that that day should overtake you as a thief: for you are all sons of light, and sons of the day: we are not of the night, nor of darkness; so then let us not sleep, as do the rest, but let us watch and be sober." He continues regarding the behavior that should be exhibited regardless of the changing and difficult times. In I Thessalonians 5:14-15, "And we exhort you…admonish the disorderly, encourage the fainthearted, support the weak, be long-suffering toward all. See that none render unto anyone evil for evil; but always follow after that which is good, one toward another, and toward all." The external events occurring within the culture should not contribute to any change of our godly and righteous behavior. We are spiritually and positionally in Christ and He is in us.

An additional word in II Peter 3:10-14 gives this description, "But the day of the Lord will come as a thief; in which the heavens shall pass away with a great noise, and the elements shall be dissolved with fervent heat, and the earth and the works that are therein shall be burned up. Seeing that these things are thus all to be dissolved, what manner of persons ought you to be in all holy living and godliness, looking for and earnestly desiring the coming of the day of God, by reason of which the heavens being on fire shall be dissolved, and the elements shall melt with fervent heat? But, according to his promise, we look for new heavens and a new earth, wherein dwells righteousness. Wherefore…seeing that you look for these things, give diligence that ye may be found in peace, without spot and blameless in his sight."

May God grant us the fortitude and confidence, as well as His grace and strength that will enable us to "give diligence that you may be found in peace, without spot and blameless in his sight." He has promised to be with us and never to forsake us. That is our hope, confidence, peace and joy. Be faithful to Him in all things and at all times. Despite a life marked by ill health, in 1925 Thomas Chisholm penned the words to:

> Great Is Thy faithfulness, O God my Father!
> There is no shadow of turning with Thee;

Trending Toward Cultural Captivity

> Thou changest not, Thy compassions, they fail not
> As Thou hast been Thou forever wilt be.

We should be challenged to a renewed commitment by the words of a young African Pastor who was martyred. Found in his coat pocket was this testimony: "I'm a part of the fellowship of the unashamed. The die has been cast. I have stepped over the line. The decision has been made. I'm a disciple of His and I won't look back, let up, slow down, back away, or be still. My past is redeemed. My present makes sense. My future is secure…My road may be narrow, my way rough, my companions few, but my guide is reliable and my mission is clear. I will not be bought, com-promised, detoured, lured away, turned back, deluded or delayed. I will not flinch in the face of sacrifice or hesitate in the presence of the adversary. I will not negotiate at the table of the enemy…I won't give up, shut up, or let up…I am a disciple of Jesus. I must give until I drop, preach until all know, and work until He comes. And when He does come for His own, He'll have no problems recognizing me. My colors will be clear!" May his tribe increase and may we be found with this level of commitment to our Lord and Savior Jesus Christ. Amen!

About the Author

I, the third of three children, was born in Brooklyn, New York and lived the first 20 years of my life there. In late Spring and Summer of 1954, I volunteered to be a worker at Lakeside Bible Conference in Carmel, New York. During the summer, I met several people who were already in a Bible College or preparing to enter their Freshman year. I stayed in a two-man cabin with a man who was President of the Student Body at Columbia Bible College (now Columbia International University) in Columbia, South Carolina. We had been assigned to work with teenagers from New York City. However, during the course of the summer, my roommate would frequently ask me whether or not I had ever thought about what God's will and plan for my life might be. His question "bugged" me and I did my best to avoid him and the question.

At the end of the summer, some friends who had pre-enrolled at Columbia Bible College ,invited me to ride to South Carolina with them and then to hitch-hike back home. I had no other plans and decided to go with them. Just to "kill time" I sat in the Orientation Sessions. When I declined to receive the sheets that were distributed, a Staff Member asked me: "Why?" I indicated that I was not a student and had not enrolled. I indicated that I would be hitchhiking back to New York once the classes began. In a very gentle way, the Staff Member indicated that if I enrolled, he and others would pray with and for me that God would provide all that was needed so I could attend the Bible College. I decided to do that and enrolled as a College Freshman. I not only received an excellent Biblical Education but in the Spring Semester (1955) one of the entering women students from Chattanooga, Tennessee arrived as a student. In the providence of God, she became my wife in 1956.

In 1958, I transferred to a new Presbyterian school, Covenant College (in St. Louis, MO, now on Lookout Mountain, GA). After graduation in 1960, I enrolled in Covenant Theological Seminary and completed my studies there in 1964. After graduation,

I was called to serve as Pastor in New Jersey. I have served as a Pastor in various places in different states continuously for more than 50 years.

A young man from one of those Pastorates is now the owner of Theocentric Publishing Group. It has been with his encouragement that I have written some books and had them published by Theocentric. Two of the more recent books published are: Taking A Serious God Seriously, and Amid The Cultural Chaos. These and other titles are available through Theocentric or Amazon.

www.ingramcontent.com/pod-product-compliance
Lightning Source LLC
Chambersburg PA
CBHW061949070426
42450CB00007BA/1097